THE LONGEST HOP

CELEBRATING 50 YEARS OF THE QANTAS KANGAROO ROUTE

1947–1997

THE LONGEST HOP

CELEBRATING 50 YEARS OF THE QANTAS KANGAROO ROUTE

1947–1997

SYDNEY · LONDON

JOHN STACKHOUSE

WITH ASSISTANCE FROM

JAMES MURRAY, BERNARD SHIRLEY, JULIAN GREEN, GEORGE ROBERTS AND OTHERS

ERNEST HENRY ALDIS, OBE, 1915–1997

In August 1997 Qantas lost a valued part of its history with the passing of Ern Aldis. Ern spent a lifetime in aviation. He began his career as an apprentice aircraft engineer to the legendary Charles Kingsford Smith before joining Qantas in 1938. He reached the pinnacle of his career when he became maintenance director. Following his retirement, Ern continued his association with the airline, volunteering his time to the Qantas Historical Collection in Sydney.

Ern Aldis witnessed the introduction of the flying boats, the Constellation and the jet era. People such as Ern have made a tremendous contribution to Qantas, and to the colour, passion and personality that marked its formative years. He will be greatly missed.

FOCUS PUBLISHING
Pty Ltd

Enquiries should be addressed to the publisher:
Focus Publishing Pty Ltd
ACN 003 600 360
PO Box 518, Edgecliff NSW 2027
Telephone: (02) 9327 4777
Fax: (02) 9362 3753
Email: focus@focus.com.au
Internet: //www.focus.com.au/

Chairman: Steven Rich
Publisher: Jaqui Lane
Managing Editor: Clare Wallis
Project Manager: William E Munt
Production Manager: Timothy Ho
Client Services Co-ordinator: Rebecca Lowrey
Assistant Editor: Anna Sanders
Designer: Patricia Ansell

ISBN 1-857359-36-2

CONTENTS

INTRODUCTION

The sleek Lockheed Constellation 749 taxied out through the drizzling darkness of a sultry Sydney night on 1 December 1947 for the first fully Qantas operated service to London.

More than 1,000 people—official guests, airline staff and onlookers—were there to farewell the 11 crew and 29 passengers taking part in the beginning of a new era in Australian air travel.

There was excitement in the air. Even rain could not dampen their spirits as they watched the lights of Mascot Airport sparkle along the silver fuselage and glisten on the faces of the pilots in the cockpit.

Earlier, they had listened politely as the Minister for Civil Aviation, Mr Drakeford, noted with good-humoured irony that apparently some people regarded 'all air travel as a luxury which ought to be heavily taxed!'

They had clapped as the aircraft's powerful engines roared into life with their characteristic cloud of blue smoke.

And they cheered as the *Charles Kingsford Smith* gathered speed and lifted off into the drizzle, carrying 2,000 lbs of food parcels for Britain which was suffering postwar shortages during a bitterly cold winter.

Mist trailed away behind the four engines, lingering for a while in the humid summer air as the Constellation climbed towards its cruising altitude.

For Qantas—and Australia—a moment in history had arrived.

The Constellation changed the level of Australia's accessibility to the world at large. The new aircraft brought comfort and glamour, with reclining seats and bunk beds, and for the first time, a pressurised cabin.

It did not, like so many aircraft of the time, have warplane aspects. Civil modifications of British military aircraft such as the Lancaster bomber (which became the Lancastrian) for example, could not disguise their origins because they were designed totally for war. Although ostensibly developed as a military transport, the Lockheed Constellation was designed with civilian passengers in mind.

With its technology and comfort, the Constellation made a successful commercial reality of what had been a more or less whimsical nickname for the flight path over Asia to Britain — the Kangaroo Route.

Not that there was anything instantaneous about the quantum leap. As early as 1941, when Qantas was caught up in the exigencies of World War II, a well-informed executive, Lester Brain, was reporting on the Constellation as a peacetime prospect:

'The outstanding machine apparently being developed for postwar commercial use is the Lockheed Constellation. This I understand to be a four-engine pressure cabin landplane said to have a range of 4,000 miles with 64 passengers.'

Brain's information was substantially accurate. The Constellation became the main instrument for the transformation of air travel in the post-war world.

The Longest Hop focuses on the 50 years since that inaugural flight, a period also covered in our companion work ... *from the dawn of aviation: The Qantas Story 1920–1995.*

These histories will surely inspire present and future Qantas staff at every level from boardroom to tarmac, to match and indeed surpass the achievements of their predecessors.

Qantas passengers will learn that they are protected by an historic continuum of care and service which derives from the extraordinary genesis of Qantas in outback Queensland where the day-to-day challenges bred a necessary caution.

Not only did the Qantas genesis create an enviable reputation for service with reliability but a catalytic linkage with the world economy of inestimable benefit to Australia.

As history shows, the airline believes that if records are made to be broken, promises are made to be kept.

James Strong

JAMES STRONG
Managing Director, Qantas Airways Ltd

IN THE BEGINNING

Pilot Hudson Fysh.
3.10.22

QUEENSLAND'S FIRST AERIAL MAIL WELCOMED
AT WINTON NOV. 1922.

The Qantas Kangaroo Route began with an Empire connection that predated the airline. The Australian Prime Minister, William (Billy) Hughes, in London for peace talks at the end of the World War I in early 1919, offered £10,000 for the 'first successful flight to Australia from Great Britain in a machine manned by Australians'.

Three young Australians, who had served in the Australian Imperial Force, decided to try for the prize. Paul McGinness and W Hudson Fysh, who had both transferred to the No. 1 Squadron of the Australian Flying Corps (AFC) together, teamed with their aircraft engineer, Arthur Baird, to enter the challenge. However, when the sponsor of their venture died before he could sign the cheque, the team was forced to withdraw.

A chance meeting one year later between McGinness and a wealthy grazier, Fergus McMaster, sowed the seeds for the development of air services in the remote rural areas of northern Australia. McMaster put his weight behind selling shares in the enterprise and after raising the capital to provide a modest foundation for its operations. Q.A.N.T.A.S. (Queensland and Northern Territory Aerial Services Ltd) was registered on 16 November 1920.

With two small and seemingly fragile biplanes, McGinness and Baird operated joyrides, demonstration flights and taxi services as a prelude to regular air mail and passenger flights. The airline's first scheduled flight took to the air on 2 November 1922, under the command of P J (Ginty) McGinness. The route from Charleville to Winton, McKinley and Cloncurry via Longreach would form the genesis of the fledgling airline's long-term ambition of creating an air service to England from Darwin.

BATTLING THE CLIMATE

The outback was a harsh teacher to the infant airline. For most of the year, temperatures were so high that the thin air robbed the engines of power and the wings of lift. The heat also created turbulence that, at best, was severely uncomfortable, at worst, dangerous. As a result, most flights began at first light and landed before eleven in the morning. Crew and passengers waited out the heat of the day in the hospitality of a station property or on the veranda of a pub in one of the towns along the route. Careful maintenance to ensure maximum reliability became the cornerstone of the company's continued operation.

As the airline grew, so too did its dream of flying the Empire Route (as it came to be known) from Australia to London. By 1934 Qantas was ready.

McMaster and Fysh looked for an alliance with Britain's flag carrier, Imperial Airways (later British Overseas Airways Corporation, then British Airways). Q.A.N.T.A.S. and Imperial formed Qantas Empire Airways (QEA). The Australian Government awarded QEA the route for its plans to operate four-engine de Havilland 86 aircraft from Brisbane and later

ABOVE: Brisbane–Singapore air service summer timetable, 1935.
BELOW: Qantas Empire Airways, Brisbane–Darwin section, 1934.

the four-engine Short S23 'C'-class Empire flying boats from Sydney.

The DH86 Commonwealth airliners flew only by day and could carry two crew and up to 10 passengers, although priority was given to air mail. They overnighted at Longreach, Darwin and Lombok Island (in Indonesia), en route to Singapore.

The Empire Route was from Brisbane to Darwin, then through what is now Indonesia to Singapore, where the passengers joined an Imperial Airways flight for the journey across Asia and Europe.

Darwin became the gateway to Australia as the Qantas planes passed through. The Timor Sea between there and Kupang enabled pilots to track their progress by the changing colour of the sea.

By 1938, Qantas had moved its headquarters to Rose Bay, Sydney, and the brief but glorious flying boat era began. The S23 Empire-class flying boats were a huge advance, technically and in terms of comfort. For the first time, Qantas was to use advanced equipment, such as an automatic pilot. Qantas introduced cabin service, replicating—as closely as possible—the service enjoyed on the great ocean liners. The airline recruited from Imperial Airways its first steward, Bill Drury, who was to train the initial crews and set the standards.

SERVICE WITH A SMILE

Qantas introduced its first in-flight service on 5 July 1938, impressing passengers from the first day. The stewards served extravagant three-course dinners that had been cooked on the ground and kept in vacuum flasks.

While in-flight cabin service kept passengers happy, new notions of marketing were striving to attract passengers away from established shipping services.

For the 17 passengers the flying boats were roomy, and had the bonus of a promenade view passing at about 240 kilometres per hour.

While QEA owned its flying boats, they were interchangeable with the British ones, since Imperial was a 50 per cent shareholder. And, like their predecessors the DH86s, the Empire boats did not fly to London with Australian crews. Initially QEA handed over to Imperial crews in Singapore (although during the early part of the war some flights went through to Karachi), while the Australians flew the British-owned aircraft south to Sydney.

The flying boats took off in the mornings from Sydney, overnighting in Townsville. After a dawn departure, the aircraft flew overland to Karumba on the Gulf of Carpentaria, with a refuelling stop at Groote Eylandt before the last domestic leg to Darwin.

Australia behind them, the flying boats journeyed on to Kupang, Bima on Flores Island, in the middle of the Indonesian archipelago, and with another overnight halt at Surabaya. On the final day, the passengers would enjoy the brief halt at Tanjong Priok, the port for Batavia (now Jakarta) before the final leg to Singapore. These leisurely days of flight ended abruptly when war came to the Pacific in 1941.

ABOVE: Qantas Empire Airways, Darwin–Singapore section.
LEFT: Interior Qantas Workshop, Surabaya. *Left to right:* McLeod, Jenkins and Hodge.

A NEW QANTAS EMERGES

CHAPTER ONE

The bombing of Singapore on 8 December 1941 brought dramatic changes to Qantas.

The bombing of Singapore on 8 December 1941 brought dramatic changes to Qantas.

The preceding 12 months had been very successful for the three-and-half-year-old flying-boat service; the big C-class Empire boats had carried 7,600 passengers, 260 tons of freight and 296 tons of mail between Sydney and Singapore.

While Singapore had originally been the point at which the Australian QEA crews handed over to Imperial/BOAC crews, as a result of the war the Australians were flying the 12,900 kilometres to Karachi. In the face of the Japanese threat, the route started to unravel. Flights to Penang in Malaysia and Bangkok stopped, but services continued—dipping southwards from Rangoon through southern Burma and Indonesia— to Singapore. Qantas started evacuating civilians from the area and soon had to pull out of Singapore during the day.

In early February the last two flying boats, which had been at the Indian end of the route, came straggling in, while Qantas and the Royal Netherlands Air Force set up an evacuation shuttle from Tjilatjap in south-eastern Java to Broome, Western Australia. The last service from Batavia, under Captain Lew Ambrose, left on 19 February 1942.

That same day, the war came to Australia. The main force of the Japanese carrier group which had struck at Pearl Harbor on 7 December raided Darwin, destroying an empty Qantas hangar after devastating the port.

ABOVE: A poster depicting the romance of the flying-boat era, produced for the 70th anniversary of Qantas in 1990.
OPPOSITE PAGE: Short Bros S23 'C' Class Empire Flying Boat *Carpentaria* VH-ABA under service at the flying boat base in Rose Bay, Sydney, 1940.

THE CASUALTIES OF WAR

By early March Qantas had lost three flying boats, and all its land planes and flying boats were on war service. The airline was evacuating civilians from the New Guinea highlands and rescuing pilots and sailors from the sea around northern Australia and Papua New Guinea. In 1942 the US forces made some Lockheed Lodestars available. These were the first American aircraft Qantas had operated and crews took them into front-line supply drops in Papua. During 1942 Qantas lost three aircraft to the war effort and three more flying boats, under charter to the RAAF, on wartime operations.

At this sombre time, the expertise and patronage of BOAC were to save the international role for Qantas. It would also pave the way for its re-emergence after the war and, indirectly, for the 1947 Constellation service.

The flame of the Empire Route was burning in Sydney where Hudson Fysh tried to muster support for a service across the Indian Ocean to link Australia with the remaining base of British power in India. BOAC also wanted to reopen the route. In 1942, however, the Civil Aviation Department rebuffed Fysh and chided him for daring to push the concept. In London, Walter Runciman, chief executive at BOAC, also supported the idea of a service across the 5,620 kilometres between Perth and Lake Koggala in Ceylon (now Sri Lanka). Working through the British Government, BOAC

ABOVE: The flying-boat era was an important phase in the development of Qantas. Here, Australian troops disembark the flying boat *Coriolanus* at Port Moresby in 1943. The Short Empire Flying Boat played a vital role during the war, carrying troops and vital supplies to and from the front line.

obtained an initial four (one more followed) Catalina flying boats and flew them to Ceylon, where Captain Bill Crowther and his Australian crews picked them up. The flights started in July 1943. The service was to become one of the epics of civil aviation.

Flying in secrecy and radio silence to avoid discovery by the enemy over the Indian Ocean, the flights took more than 24 hours—in one case 32 hours. The Catalinas, overloaded with mail, priority passengers and fuel for the long journey, were entirely dependent on celestial navigation.

ABOVE: Wounded Australian troops from the Buna-Gona campaign about to embark on a Qantas Lockheed Lodestar at Dobodura in Papua New Guinea during 1942.
BELOW: Memories of the war years.

THE KANGAROO ROUTE

The Catalinas reopened the Australia-to-Britain air route. The ground crews which improved and maintained the aircraft for these flights, then the longest scheduled sector in the world, installed a slipway, nose hangar and workshop on the bank of the Swan River at Nedlands near Perth. They were then able to haul the flying boats out of the water and work on the engines under cover while the rest of the aircraft was in the open. At times they had to scrounge spares and parts to keep the Catalinas flying. To improve efficiency and reliability for the long flight, the original American-built engines were replaced by Australian-made Pratt and Whitneys of a similar type. Proud of their work, they hoisted a sign alongside the hangar saying 'Kangaroo Route'. The name stuck and a new game had begun.

At one stage Qantas had almost no aircraft and a surplus of pilots. While its workshops were buzzing with war-effort repair work, the identity of the airline itself was threatened. The inauguration of the historic Indian Ocean services in June 1943 gave Qantas a new sense of purpose, later continuing to Karachi.

RIGHT: Qantas war worker,
Rose Bay, Sydney, July 1944.

In June 1944 Qantas received its first Consolidated Liberator, a transport version of the bomber, and put it on the route between Perth and Colombo, via Learmonth in northern Western Australia. A second aircraft arrived in August. The fleet built up quickly with a third in December 1945 and a fourth in March 1946. The flight from Perth to Learmonth took three hours and 40 minutes, the Indian Ocean crossing another 16 hours and 13 minutes. The Catalina services were to end in July 1945, after completing 271 crossings covering just on one million miles (1.6 million kilometres).

After World War II, the Kangaroo Route was maintained by later types of Short Brothers, Hythes and Sandringham flying boats, and Lancastrians. The 'Lanc' would typically carry six passengers and high-priority mails. At first the route was from Sydney to Learmonth, Ratmalana (Ceylon) and Karachi (where the Australian crew handed over to the British), then to Lydda in Palestine and Hurn, now a Royal Air Force base on the outskirts of Bournemouth, in southern England. Later they operated from Sydney via Darwin to Singapore for a night-stop, then via Calcutta to Karachi, where Qantas crews handed over to BOAC crews. The route was then to Lydda and London.

Lancastrians, as converted Lancasters, could only carry passengers at up to 10,000 feet. They were also noisy. Passengers had to perch on seats that ran down one side of the aircraft, facing windows that went down the other side. The single steward aboard

THE LONGEST HOP

had to hop and skip down the narrow cabin, stepping over a wing girder halfway down and trying to avoid tripping as he served food and drinks in crude containers. The seats were converted into six bunks for passengers at night.

The flying boats operated a more leisurely, alternative service. BOAC had introduced the Hythe class.

Inside, the Hythes were even more spacious than the original Empire boats. They carried 16 passengers in a number of cabins, and each passenger could have a bunk. They also had a longer range and were slightly faster (almost 270 kilometres per hour, about the speed of a DC3), so the previous nine-day journey to London took only a week. After departing Sydney at night, the Hythes flew to Bowen in Queensland to refuel. They were able to fly the 2,030 kilometre journey across Australia from Bowen to Darwin (a night-stop) in a single hop, then to Surabaya and Singapore for another overnight. They went to Rangoon, for another stop, Calcutta and Karachi (night-stop), and on to Cairo via Basra. There was one more halt in North Africa before the flight continued to London, via Marseilles.

Although the Hythe boats were not pressurised, they flew higher than most previous aircraft. Writer Frank Clune in his book *High-Ho to London* describes how after Darwin, his aircraft began to climb to 10,000 feet (about 3,000 metres), 'partly to obtain favourable winds, partly to get above the clouds and partly to keep out of the way of the numerous mountain peaks, which project from the archipelago's various isles. As we neared Lombok, I found breathing difficult and

ABOVE: A QEA promotional poster featuring a flying boat over Sydney Harbour.

The famous Raffles Hotel in Singapore, photographed c. 1940. Qantas passengers and some crew stayed here en route to London.

THE LONGEST HOP

realised the pilot was going higher to dodge Mount Rinjani, 12,261 feet [about 3,775 metres], the highest peak in Indonesia. Soon we saw the mountain about ten miles to the left of our course. Green swathed, it was ringed with a quoit of white clouds noosing its summit.'

Flying with Qantas before the war, Clune had already crossed the equator. He told how he was given and cherished a certificate, with the imprint of King Neptune and signed by the skipper, bearing witness that he had crossed the equator and taken to the skies of the northern hemisphere.

Clune, who disembarked in Surabaya in early 1947, found himself in the middle of the Dutch attempt to regain their empire. The prewar hotels had reopened. Raffles, in Singapore, where Qantas passengers and some crew stayed, was showing signs of wear, as was the other one in town, the Adelphi. The favourite for Clune, as it was with many of the Qantas transients, was the Seaview out along the east coast, with its tennis courts, nearby swimming and excellent food.

A CHANGE OF LOYALTIES

By this time Qantas was convinced that, despite its desire to 'buy British', it would have to look to the United States for its new equipment. But to do so, Qantas executives would have to overcome domestic political hurdles and international obstacles. The British aircraft industry proclaimed its intention to produce modern, postwar aircraft, yet the factories that had produced thousands of bombers and fighters could not cope with the different requirements of the new civilian airlines. Qantas reluctantly came to the conclusion that it could not survive on good intentions alone.

n the last days of the war, a British Government committee charted the future of the British industry. It called for a huge flying boat (the Princess) and a monster landplane, the Brabazon (named after Lord Brabazon, chairman of the committee) neither of which ever went into service. The plan included a four-engine, long-range turbo-prop, the Britannia, and eventually a jet aircraft, which was to become the Comet. This was envisaged more as a fast Empire mail carrier than as a passenger aircraft.

BOAC tried to coerce Qantas to buy British. Still with a mindset of the colonial era, the British Government put pressure on the Australian Government. Australia was a member of the British-led sterling bloc and was desperately short of money. While the prospect of buying British appealed to the old-fashioned loyalties of Qantas people such as Fysh and McMaster, it was a hopeless alternative for the logical minds of the technical people, such as Captains Scotty Allan and Bert Ritchie, and the cool financial brains of C O Turner and his staff.

Qantas believed that only one aircraft suited the Kangaroo Route: the Lockheed Constellation, which was faster than the proposed Tudor II and the Lancastrian. A choice became urgent when the traditional rival of Qantas, KLM Royal Dutch Airlines, announced that it would put Constellations on the Batavia route and was pressing for Australian rights.

Qantas had already been discussing contracts with Lockheed. And when Lockheed came up with a form of time payment, with 25 per cent down, the expenditure suddenly became affordable for both the airline and the Government.

Early in September 1946 the pressures came to a head. The Minister for Aviation, Arthur Drakeford, secured an appointment for Fysh to call

LEFT: The first Qantas Constellation *Ross Smith*, delivered in October 1947. The *Charles Kingsford Smith*, which made the first Sydney–London flight in December 1947 was delivered two weeks later.

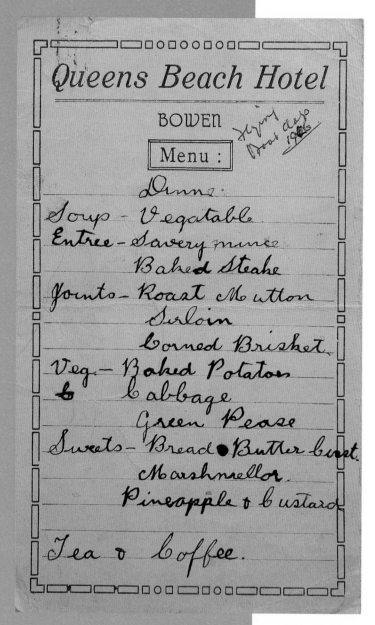

ABOVE: Menu from Queens Beach Hotel, Bowen, a Qantas stopover in north Queensland.

on the Prime Minister, who was at Victoria Barracks in Melbourne. Chifley, puffing his trademark pipe, had in front of him the flimsies of an urgent telegram. It was, the PM said, from Prime Minister Clement Attlee in London, 'begging us not to go on with those Constellations you want'. According to Fysh, Chifley paused, smiled and added: 'Well, anyhow, I've decided. We'll give it a go.'

Qantas was to choose the Lockheed Constellation, one of the most important decisions in the history of the airline. BOAC eventually followed suit. Formal authorisation to buy four aircraft arrived on 10 September, and preparations to inaugurate the first all-Australian and Constellation service to London began.

The change from 'Empire Route' to 'Kangaroo Route' flagged a change, also, in the way Australia saw itself and its links with the world. Despite Fysh's abiding admiration of BOAC and British institutions, it had become time for Qantas to fly solo.

The Australian Government nationalised Qantas and bought out the BOAC share, making it entirely government-owned. (It remained so until March 1993, when British Airways bought 25 per cent of the company in the trade sale part of the privatisation process that saw Qantas successfully floated and listed on the Australian Stock Exchange at the end of July 1995.)

Even as Qantas was planning its Constellation service, many travellers were disdainful of a schedule that would get to London in a mere four days. To a generation used to leisurely six-week boat trips, this seemed like undue haste. The nine-day journey by flying boat was a happy memory. Seven days seemed about right. But the Constellation was not only about to compress time; it was to begin a trend that saw the familiar ports and airports of the old days slide into disuse and off the beaten air track. Today Bowen, Surabaya, Rangoon and many other former stops are merely memories that pass virtually unnoticed beneath an aircraft on long, non-stop flights.

BELOW: Arrival of first Qantas Constellation *Ross Smith* at Kingsford Smith Airport, Sydney, after flying from Burbank, California, in an elapsed time of 43 hours. The Minister for Civil Aviation, Mr Drakeford, below, welcomed the aircraft.
INSET: *Aeroplane* magazine, London, records the arrival of Constellation *Ross Smith* on the first all-Qantas operated proving flight to London in November 1947.

NEW BOY ARRIVES.—"Ross Smith," Q.E.A.'s first Lockheed Constellation 749 arriving at London Airport on November 21 at the end of a proving flight from Australia. First arrival on the scheduled service will reach London on December 5 from Sydney. During December the service will be operated at a once-weekly frequency which will be stepped up to six flights a month in January. The aircraft will all be fitted with "Speedpaks" as shown in this photograph.
"Aeroplane" photograph

THE FIRST HOP

Three hours after taking off from Sydney's Mascot Airport late on the night of 1 December 1947, the Qantas Lockheed 749 Constellation was well on its way to Darwin...

24

Three hours after taking off from Sydney's Mascot Airport late on the night of 1 December 1947, the Qantas Lockheed 749 Constellation was well on its way to Darwin, in Australia's Northern Territory. This was the first scheduled Qantas flight to London of an Australian-owned aircraft with Australian crews.

The official length of the route was 11,956 miles (about 19,130 kilometres). The elapsed time from Sydney to London was 93.5 hours and the return journey took 84 hours. The flight time was about 56 hours. This compared with a week for the flying boats, which made 14 intermediate stops between Sydney and London, with four or five overnights. The length of the flying-boat journey was 12,287 miles (19,660 kilometres) and the time spent in the air was 83 hours. Even the 3,500-kilometre non-stop first sector to Darwin was a big advance on the first international flights from Sydney a decade before, when the flying boats had taken two days to creep around the eastern and northern coasts to reach the Northern Territory capital. Qantas had been using Darwin since 1934 as its departure point for the world.

At about half past one, the cabin lights in the Constellation were dimmed. The three stewards had finished serving drinks and a late supper to the 29 passengers and were resting before they had to serve tea and coffee prior to the aircraft's arrival in Darwin soon after dawn. They were aware of what this flight was carrying in its hold. Qantas staff had donated the money to buy 2,000 pounds (about 910 kilograms) of food parcels for their colleagues in BOAC. Britain was undergoing a dark and cold winter, and the gesture was typical of Australian regard for what many, in those days, still called 'the mother country'.

The front end of the aircraft was a scene of subdued activity. The

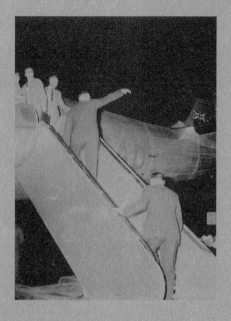

ABOVE: First flight, aircraft boarding. BELOW: Chairman and managing director, Hudson Fysh (later Sir Hudson), hands the official mail bag to Captain K G Jackson before the departure. OPPOSITE: Minister for Civil Aviation, Mr Drakeford, cuts a red, white and blue ribbon to mark the commencement of the new Kangaroo Route service to London.

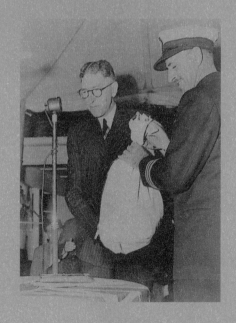

A CHILDHOOD MEMORY

'Imagine if you can the excitement I felt as a six-year-old boy arriving at Heathrow Airport, London, on 5 December 1947, a cold winter's day with snow on the ground, preparing to fly to Australia on a big silver plane called a Constellation.

'Never before had I been near a plane but here I was, my mum and younger brother climbing up this high stairway into the unknown. The feelings of anticipation and curiosity experienced by a young boy about to fly come back to me quite vividly even now.

'We flew via Zurich, Calcutta and Karachi before arriving in Singapore. On the way I played with my new dinky toys bought specifically for the trip and drank drinks provided by the crew from thermos flasks. Nothing could prepare us for the heat of the tropics nor Raffles Hotel. The bedroom was huge with a big fan rotating slowly on the ceiling. The bed had no blankets, just a sheet.

'Then on to Sydney, where we spent a few days at Bondi Beach before the three of us boarded a sea plane to continue our flight to New Zealand. This, however, is another story.

'Looking back on this great adventure 50 years ago, I know why I still love flying. Thank you, Qantas.'

Roger C V Eames

navigator, Alan Hughes, had plotted the last radio beacon at Walgett, New South Wales, and did not expect any more navigation aids until reaching the Darwin area—1,500 kilometres ahead. Over the Australian emptiness, Hughes had been using his sextant to plot the aircraft's position. He moved forward to the flight deck to pass the position and unchanged course to the skipper, Captain Ken Jackson, and his first officer, another experienced Qantas captain, Bert Yates. A third pilot, Captain Jim Pollock, was aft in the front seat of the cabin, reserved for crew rest, having a brief nap before it was his turn to relieve. Radio operator Bruce Beresford tapped out a routine position report and weather information on his Morse key.

The four big Wright Cyclone engines were running smoothly as flight engineer D E Brown monitored them on the maze of instruments on his panel. So far, there hadn't been any real problems with either the engines or the systems. He suspected that one of the cylinders in Number 3 wasn't delivering full power, so he jotted a note in his logbook for the ground staff in Darwin and warned the captain, even if no action was needed immediately.

Ken Jackson checked the instruments for the air-conditioning and pressurisation of the cabin. From a technical point of view, engineer Brown wondered whether this complication was merited. But it made all the difference for passengers—to be able to fly smoothly through the night

ABOVE: A celebration of flying with Qantas over the Indian Ocean from Perth to Ceylon, more commonly known as the 'Kangaroo Service'.

The delivery flight of the fourth Lockheed 749 Constellation *Charles Kingsford Smith* at Mascot in 1947. *From left:* Sir Hudson Fysh; Captain Allan Furze; Captain Joe Towle (then Lockheed's director of flight tests); Bill Nielson; Captain R J Bert Ritchie (general manager) and Captain G U 'Scotty' Allan (who went on to become deputy general manager).

at 18,000 feet (more than three miles above the arid interior of the continent), way above the bad weather that had marked their departure.

As they cruised over 'the Corner' where South Australia and Queensland meet, they were only 500 kilometres to the west of Charleville. This was where, before dawn, almost 25 years previously, the first Qantas scheduled service had lifted off the ground, a single-engined wood-and-fabric biplane, on a flight to Longreach, with another sector to Winton, McKinley and Cloncurry the next day. The Constellation—designed to fly at 300 miles (480 kilometres) per hour—could have flown that pioneering route in less than two hours.

THE LONGEST AIR ROUTE

It had been a long journey for the infant Qantas from Longreach to a world that was opening up for the airline. That non-stop night flight inaugurated what was to become the longest air route in existence.

The flight marked the postwar beginnings of Qantas as a major airline. Within just a few years, it would grow to be one of the 10 biggest air carriers in the world and an influential player in the politics of the air transport industry.

The service was built on two great traditions. One was airmanship; the other was an uncompromising approach to maintenance and engineering. The goal of those in the air and those who served on the ground was simple: safety and reliability.

The symbolism of their location would not have been lost on the Constellation's veteran crew, locked in a pressurised fuselage as they cruised high over the Australian outback on that December morning in 1947.

Clockwise from left: Captain
Bert Ritchie; Constellation
Lawrence Hargrave; a
Constellation Navigator; the
astro compass; navigational
instruments.

NAVIGATION

In some respects, flying the
Constellation on the world's
longest scheduled air route
50 years ago called on
navigational skills and
technologies that Captain
James Cook would have
found familiar on the
Endeavour in 1769–70.

The Constellation crews
were virtually on their own,
their only connection to the
air traffic system the dots
and dashes of hand-
transmitted Morse and the
ears of the radio operators.

30

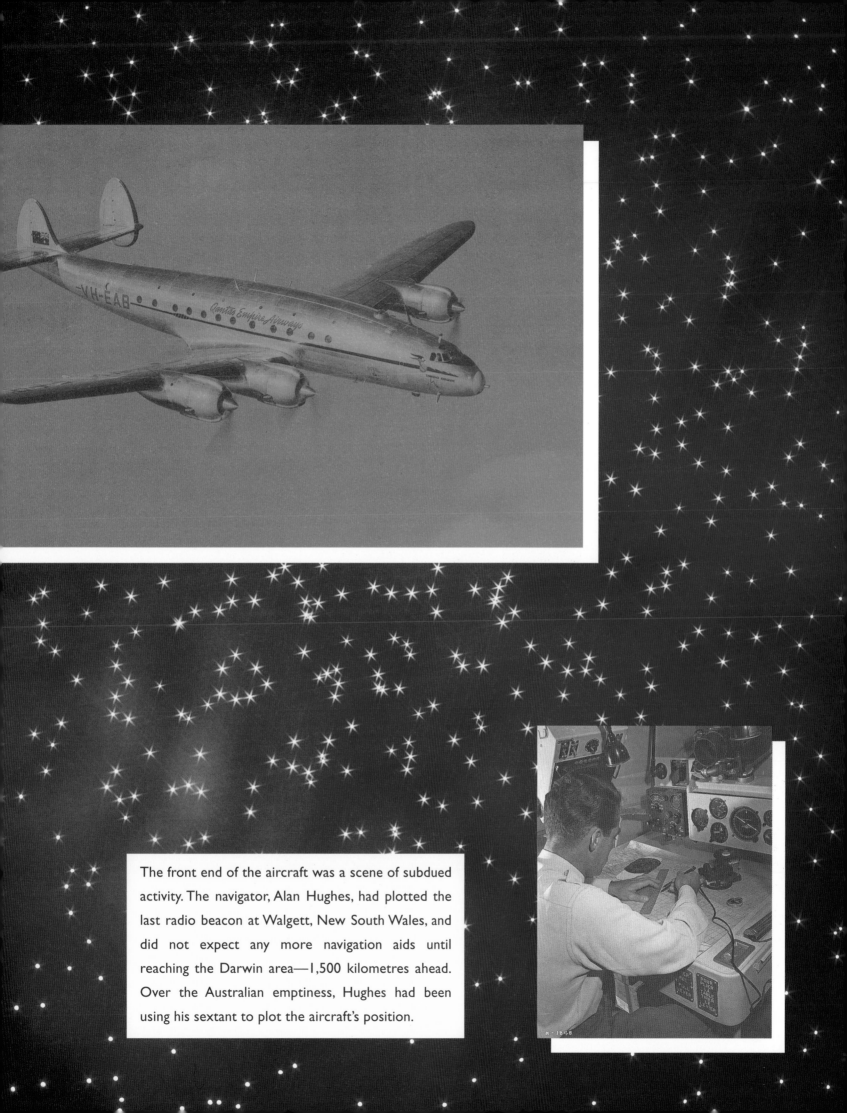

The front end of the aircraft was a scene of subdued activity. The navigator, Alan Hughes, had plotted the last radio beacon at Walgett, New South Wales, and did not expect any more navigation aids until reaching the Darwin area—1,500 kilometres ahead. Over the Australian emptiness, Hughes had been using his sextant to plot the aircraft's position.

This view of the Lockheed flightline at Burbank shows the L1049 Super Constellation (foreground) and its predecessor, the L749 Constellation. At rear is the giant R60-1 Constitution, developed by Lockheed for the US Navy as a long-range troop carrier. It could carry up to 168 passengers on two decks in a fully pressurised fuselage.

LOCKHEED

THE HOWARD HUGHES CONSTELLATION

Even before it had left the drawing board, Lockheed's sleek-lined Constellation airliner was touched by the glitter of the movies. Lockheed's design studios and factory were at suburban Burbank Airport in Los Angeles, not far from Hollywood. The link was Howard Hughes, who—as a pilot and a producer—bridged the worlds of aviation and the silver screen. The Constellation was built to his specification for a transcontinental airliner. Hughes backed his dream with his own millions and, on its delivery flight, broke all the coast-to-coast records.

Hughes, the heir to one of the biggest fortunes in the United States, was a graduate of the prestigious California Institute of Technology who had begun flying when he was 14. In the 1930s he set several international and national aviation records, including a round-the-world time. The Hughes wealth came from the petroleum industry. At the age of 19, Howard had inherited the Hughes Tool Co. Later he moved into film production, and produced RKO Radio movies that were star-studded successes. He went on to acquire real estate, hotels and gambling casinos in Nevada.

In 1939 Hughes bought 46 per cent of the stock of Transcontinental & Western Airlines (later to become TWA). Like all American airlines at that time, TWA was eager to take advantage of the technologies that military spending was creating. But Hughes wanted aircraft that were designed specifically for civilian air transport. He defined his dream aircraft as being able to fly from the west coast of America to the east, carrying a payload of 6,000 pounds (2,730 kilograms) non-stop at a speed of 300 miles (480 kilometres) per hour. Prospective financiers recoiled from the risk, as did most of the manufacturers. Hughes undertook to bankroll the new aircraft from his own private fortune. And it was at Lockheed that Hughes found enthusiasm for the proposal.

ABOVE: Burbank was a busy Los Angeles airport as well as home to Lockheed.

Lockheed's special projects unit, the famous 'Skunk Works', had just finished designing the twin-boom P38 Lightning, which was to emerge as one of the finest long-range fighters in the rapidly approaching war. The wing that Lockheed had developed for the fighter could be scaled up to become a wing for a high-speed airliner. At that time, the speeds Hughes wanted for his civilian transport were about the same as those the air forces of the world were getting from their front-line fighters.

Lockheed had also been talking to Pan American and was working quietly on a wooden mock-up of an aircraft called the Excalibur, in which the US Navy was also interested. But the TWA team ruled it out, as proposed, because they feared that it would be too heavy and under-powered. Hughes, together with a group of TWA engineers and pilots, asked Lockheed to redevelop the design incorporating huge new power plants developed by the Wright company for the army.

34

W hen Hughes took over the Excalibur project, he imposed his characteristic secrecy, moving the designers into an isolated villa until the contract was signed in July 1939. The aircraft was redesignated 'Constellation' (Lockheed aircraft often had star-related names—'Vega' and 'Orion' among them).

The Constellation, in model form, 'flew' for hundreds of hours in wind tunnels. The result was probably the most beautiful passenger airliner ever built. Designated the 'Lockheed 49' (later 049), it could carry up to 64 passengers in an economy (coach) configuration.

Pan Am learned of the Constellation project and asked to participate. Its version was to have longer range, provision for a radio operator and a navigator, and an astrodome for taking sights in the top of the fuselage. This was designated the '149' and provided the base model for the 749 series that Qantas was to buy. TWA and Pan Am each ordered 40 aircraft for delivery in 1942. But this was not to happen.

The United States Government imposed priorities on building military aircraft as the war flared up in Europe and after December 1941, when America entered the war, production of civilian aircraft was halted.

The military awarded priority to the Douglas C54 (DC4 was the designation applied to civil version of the C54) as its four-engined workhorse, which entered service in increasing numbers after mid-1942. Hughes and TWA lobbied hard for the Constellation project to continue and the military eventually agreed, giving it the transport designation 'C69'. The agreement was that Hughes would pay for the prototype, take delivery, then sell it at cost to the military. The orders for a total of 80 aircraft would go ahead but they would be delivered as military transports.

ABOVE: Howard Hughes, multi-millionaire movie producer and pilot, at the Chicago Municipal Airport, in 1936, preparing for a flight to Los Angeles, California, in which he hoped to set a speed record. BELOW: Hughes and Ava Gardner are shown at ringside during the title bout between heavyweight champion Joe Louis and Tami Auriello in Yankee Stadium, 10 September 1946. Hughes had recently left a hospital, where he was being treated for injuries received in the crash of his experimental plane.

Howard Hughes (1905–1976), flew over New York in his Lockheed 10 aircraft in 1938 at the start of a round-the-world flight which lasted four days.

ughes kept in close touch with the project. Ground tests of the prototype began in November 1942 and flight testing in April 1943. The aircraft handed over to Hughes to deliver on 16 April 1944 was of gleaming, bare aluminium instead of drab army olive. Cheekily, Hughes had had twin red TWA stripes painted on the fuselage, with 'The Transcontinental Line', which annoyed the military brass.

Early the following morning Hughes and his crew took off in the aircraft from Burbank Airport. A non-stop poker game began in the back, where the engineers and TWA executives were travelling. As the plane burned off fuel it climbed to 18,000 feet (about 5,455 metres) and achieved a ground speed of 385 mph (about 616 kph). The best true air speed was 313 mph, well over Hughes's dream specification. The flight to Washington DC took six hours, 58 minutes. Hughes, TWA and Lockheed were delighted with the time, which shattered all records. Rival American Airlines previously held the record of 10 hours, 23 minutes, set in 1934 by a single-engine Vultee Speedster.

With the war ending, the military decided that it no longer needed the C69 fleet and the aircraft were converted into civilian versions. Although the type had been so long in gestation, it was still little tested in civilian service, and operators quickly found bugs—some just annoying, others more serious.

While the problems were being tackled, the Constellation continued its development. Qantas executives, including Hudson Fysh as well as engineers and pilots, had either inspected or flown in the prototype or earlier versions of the Constellation. Despite its problems, they had no difficulty in recommending it as the aircraft best suited to the needs of Qantas.

DAVID McNICOLL

A distinguished war correspondent during World War II, David McNicoll was a pioneer of the opinion column format in Australia. He was editor-in-chief of Australian Consolidated Press from 1953 to 1972. His weekly column appears in *The Bulletin* magazine.

'*My memories of flying Qantas include the proving flight of the original Constellation to London with the co-founder of the airline, Hudson Fysh. On the flight various problems were sorted out. This, of course, was before the first scheduled flight from Sydney to London in 1947. Since then I have flown thousands of miles with the airline.*

'*With Qantas you have quality as well as safety. There is a wonderful feeling of being at home when you fly Qantas. You know that you are among friends, that you are comfortable and that you are being properly looked after.*'

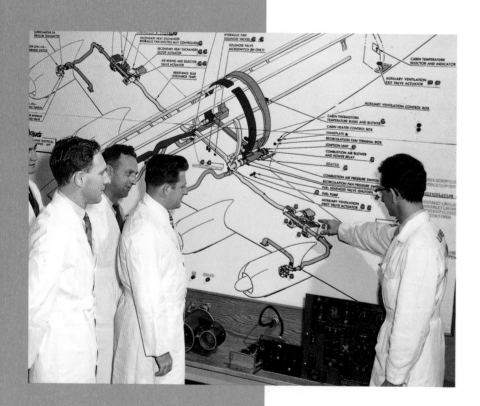

ABOVE: Qantas and BOAC ground engineers at Lockheed Ground Training School in the late 1940s. *Left to right:* Charlie Eames, N V Manning, T S Ford and the Lockheed instructor.

By this time, the weight of the aircraft had been increased and its performance improved with new engines. The result was the Lockheed 749 model, which Qantas bought. During service, in 1951 this model was upgraded again to the L749A, the final version of the 749 family.

Howard Hughes was later to suffer a bad plane crash that left him in continuous pain, and he lived the rest of his days as a recluse. But at Burbank in 1947, he was just one of the aviation pros, keenly following the progress of the airliner that had begun as a dream.

Howard Hughes shown at the controls of his 200–ton flying boat, the *Spruce Goose*, on 1 November 1947, as he prepared to taxi the big craft for the first time, in Los Angeles harbour.

A MEETING WITH HOWARD HUGHES

George A Roberts joined Qantas in 1936 when the total staff was 50. He works today as the head of the Qantas Historical Collection in Sydney.

'Following the decision by Qantas to purchase the Lockheed 749 Constellation, a number of key engineering staff were posted to the Lockheed Aircraft Corporation facility in Burbank, California, for familiarisation and training on the new technology aircraft.

'From late 1946 and throughout 1947 we met with personnel from all sections of the industry—from suppliers of major components such as the engines, propellers, hydraulics and electronics, to the airframe manufacturer itself at Burbank. Of these meetings, but under different circumstances, we encounted none other than the designer of the Constellation—Howard Hughes.

'They were casual meetings, held on a number of occasions in the cafe of the Burbank control tower, over a cup of coffee and a donut. Conversation was, I recall, initiated by our Australian accent, and was friendly but direct. He displayed a keen interest in Qantas operations down under.

'These informal meetings were frequently attended by an associate of Hughes, Paul Mantz, who engineered the transport of that other famous Howard Hughes aircraft—the Spruce Goose—from its place of manufacture well inland on the Santa Fe railroad to its destination at Long Beach, California.'

Out of a great past
a Greater Future

QANTAS
EMPIRE AIRWAYS

THE BIG NAME IN EMPIRE AVIATION

RHYS WILLIAMS

ABOVE: A poster depicting a futuristic aircraft based on the Bristol Brabazon— a long-range aircraft proposed for BOAC but which never saw service.

As Qantas aircraft started flying the Kangaroo Route, Lockheed was already looking to the future. It bought the original 049 prototype (which had come into the possession of Howard Hughes), and made in the order of 550 changes to produce the L1049, the Super Constellation, which was to be the mainstay of the Qantas fleet until the jet era.

The Lockheed Constellations made possible a safe and modern passenger service. In 1947 Qantas crews flew all the way to London for the first time, fulfilling the ambition of the airline's founders: to fly the Australian flag on the 'Empire Route'.

With the Australian-owned aircraft, the Qantas crews did not have to change in Singapore or Karachi. By inaugurating the world's longest air route an eventful quarter-century after its first flight, Qantas came of age. On the commercial side, it long retained an alliance with BOAC, and eventually, as part of its privatisation, formed a new alliance with a revitalised—and successfully privatised—British Airways in early 1993.

The December 1947 inaugural flight from Sydney to London was a watershed for Qantas. The Government was in the process of taking over the airline, firstly buying out BOAC, its long-time partner, and later the remaining private shareholders who had founded Q.A.N.T.A.S. There was also a changing of the guard. Sir Fergus McMaster, the founding chairman, was standing down because of heart trouble. Another founder, Sir Hudson Fysh, was taking on the mantle of both chairman and managing director. The relatively youthful chief accountant, C O (later Sir Cedric) Turner was making waves as he tried to straighten out the tangled financial relations with the partner on the Kangaroo Route, BOAC.

BELOW: Qantas Empire Airways Constellation *Ross Smith* at Canberra in October 1947.

ABOVE (*left to right*): Captain Bert Ritchie, Captain 'Scotty' Allan, Hudson Fysh and Captain Allan Furze.

G rowing from the professional skills of McMaster, Fysh and McGinness was an expertise in aircraft evaluation and an ability to understand and take advantage of the huge changes emanating from aviation technology after World War II. In many ways this defined the airline: being able to assess rival aircraft designs and choosing the equipment most closely matched to the needs of Qantas while delivering safety, reliability and the resulting commercial success. The era that began with the selection of the Constellation ran through the choice of Boeing jets in the 1950s and the 747 family in the early 1970s. It drove home to Qantas that aircraft evaluation and the correct choice, regardless of political and other pressures that were so often brought to bear, were the key to success.

It was no accident that this clutch of professional skills, bringing together airmanship, engineering and hard-nosed commercial instincts, was to yield three future senior executives of Qantas: Captain 'Scotty' Allan, a deputy chief executive; Captain Bert Ritchie, a chief executive; and Ron Yates, the first Australian graduate engineer to join the airline after the war, who succeeded Ritchie. They headed a strong and aggressive management team, which developed from the earlier succession of the founder, (Sir) Hudson Fysh, to the chairmanship and the emergence of C O (later Sir Cedric) Turner as managing director.

In the events leading up to the December 1947 inaugural flight, Allan was instrumental in selecting the Constellation. Ritchie, a wartime pilot, led the flying team that trained in the United States to bring the Constellation into service. And Yates, still a youngster, was to play an important role in helping organise the logistics of this first big, postwar step.

History shows that the tradition of independent evaluation and selection of aircraft was rooted in the origins of Qantas in western Queensland. The heat, the isolation, the sheer distance from factory support and the need to get best value for money were factors that led to an exhaustive evaluation process, even in the 1920s. Ultimately, in these harsh conditions, the lives of passengers and pilots depended on getting it right.

The success of the Kangaroo Route and the emergence of a strong executive team which understood the essentials of the airline business were to lay the foundation for the establishment of Qantas as a powerful international airline. Within a decade it would be first to offer a round-the-world service, and several years later became the first non-American airline to move into a new era with commercially successful jet aircraft.

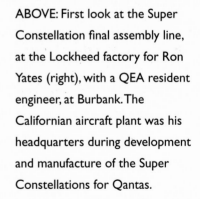

ABOVE: First look at the Super Constellation final assembly line, at the Lockheed factory for Ron Yates (right), with a QEA resident engineer, at Burbank. The Californian aircraft plant was his headquarters during development and manufacture of the Super Constellations for Qantas.

QANTAS TRANSFORMS

By 1946 Qantas had a diverse fleet of aircraft and a route structure that seemed to have grown without long-term objectives.

By 1946 Qantas had a diverse fleet of aircraft and a route structure that seemed to have grown without long-term objectives. Within 12 months, Qantas had launched its Constellation service to London and was also operating Lancastrians to Norfolk Island and Japan (via Darwin and Manila), as well as Catalinas to Lord Howe Island.

As if mirroring this chaotic equipment and route structure, the airline's future as a company was also uncertain. The Labor Government was under attack from the big unions, deemed to be under communist control. The struggles on the right and the left made it hard for the Government to conceive and develop policy.

A COMPANY UNDER STRESS

At home, Qantas was tightly stretched. Key staff had gone to the United States to train on, and learn how to maintain, the Constellations, leaving the airline poorly equipped to run its network of disparate operations. The introduction of Constellations was the most radical move Qantas had ever made. The strain—in terms of people, training, financing, setting up a new system for spares and new workshops—was at its peak when the very structure of the company was in doubt.

The following year, Qantas opened some new services to the Pacific Islands. It also surveyed a route to South Africa, which it would not inaugurate for some years.

1947–56

WORLD EVENTS

• The Korean War began in 1950 as a United Nations effort to halt the invasion of South Korea by North Korea.

• Queen Elizabeth II, accompanied by her husband, Prince Philip, Duke of Edinburgh, arrived in Australia by Qantas Constellation on 4 February 1954 for her first visit. An estimated one million people welcomed her in Sydney.

SPORT

• Don Bradman announced his retirement on 13 December 1948, the 21st anniversary of his entry into first-class cricket and after leading Australia to a 4–0 Test victory over England. He scored 6,996 runs in 52 Test innings, with an average of 99.94.

• World bantamweight champion, Jimmy Carruthers, announced his retirement on 17 May 1954, the first world champion to retire undefeated (after 19 championship bouts, four of them for the world title).

• In the 1956 Melbourne Olympics, Australia won 13 gold, eight silver and 14 bronze medals, the country's greatest performance, placing it third after the Soviet Union and the United States in the world medal count.

POP CULTURE

• Laurence Olivier and his wife Vivien Leigh were mobbed by enthusiastic supporters on the Old Vic Tour of Australia in 1948 playing in Sheridan's *School for Scandal*, Wilder's *The Skin of Our Teeth*, and Shakespeare's *Richard III*.

• Australia's first mass-produced car, the Holden, was launched in Melbourne by General Motors on 30 November 1948.

• The Australian Broadcasting Commission began its independent news service on 1 June 1947.

The ensuing period of consolidation on the Kangaroo Route showed that a fleet of only four modern aircraft could not rise to the demands of the world's longest air route. Another Constellation was hired from BOAC, which by this time had been able to overcome its government's objections to buying American aircraft. BOAC had bought Stratocruisers for the Atlantic and five Constellations from Ireland's national airline, which was unable to use them. Qantas, which wanted those aircraft (as they were available for purchase in sterling), was able to lease one as it battled for government permission to buy four more.

The route over the United States to Britain and Europe was only about 1,500 kilometres longer than the Kangaroo Route over India; and, given the international vagaries of Asia and the Middle East, many business travellers regarded it as safer. Eventually Qantas was to be awarded the Pacific services, which it called the 'Southern Cross Route', when it took delivery of the next generation of Lockheed passenger aircraft—the bigger, faster and possibly even more handsome L1049, the Super Constellation.

In these years Qantas steadily accumulated experience in flying internationally. The airline began to build up a reputation for reliability and service which even partners such as BOAC envied, developing into the Qantas we know today. The vehicle that paved the way to that success was the original Lockheed 749, the Constellation.

ABOVE: Founder, chairman and managing director, Hudson Fysh, as painted by William Dargie.
OPPOSITE PAGE: Her Majesty, Queen Elizabeth, and the Duke of Edinburgh, on arrival in Broken Hill, by Qantas Constellation, are met by Sir John Northcott, Governor of NSW, Miss Elizabeth Northcott, and Mr J Cahill, Premier of NSW.

ON THE QANTAS KANGAROO ROUTE

On the Qantas Kangaroo Route the limited number of passengers and the first-class fare (about £325 from Sydney to London, or £525 return) maximised revenue. The cost of the fare would translate nominally into $650. But in 1947, £7 was a typical weekly wage for many Australians. The wage equivalent today would be about $20,000. To take another comparison: the cost of a house was between £600 and £800, so £325 would equal half the cost of a suburban home. In modern terms, that would approximate $75,000.

In terms of either purchasing power or housing, why were fares so expensive? The price of a Constellation was about US$750,000. Each

SCOBIE BREASLEY

Arthur 'Scobie' Breasley is one of those rare sportsmen who improved with age. Born 1914 in Melbourne, he was 50 when he became Britain's champion jockey and won his first English Derby. He repeated this feat at 52. He retired from racing in 1968 after 40 years in the saddle.

'My wife May and I always enjoyed flying Qantas because it was a better all-round service and the crew were much more helpful.

'Our first trip overseas was in 1950 and we returned to Australia at the end of 1952. After that we always tried to use Qantas. Obviously, it's a long way from Australia to England and I can remember flying on board the Constellation when it had bunk accommodation and thinking, "This is a great way to beat jet lag." I liked riding winners and when I flew Qantas to or from Australia, I knew I was on another.'

aircraft was in Qantas service for a period of about seven years. The Constellation was considerably slower than any of today's jets. So its overheads were high in terms of passengers carried. Also, given the high spares usage, the aircraft was expensive to maintain.

Another factor was the crew level required to operate the aircraft. The Lockheed 749 on Qantas routes needed three pilots because of duty periods of 30 hours. Operating crews needed rest periods. There were also two flight engineers, a navigator and a radio officer (all long-distance communications were in Morse). There was a cabin crew of three for a total of 10. In the early days crews would be 'slipped' between flights in Singapore and Karachi, staying in hotels or hostels, with other crews turning around in London. They could wait three or four days between flights until route frequencies built up. All this made for an expensive operation.

Compare today's economics. A Boeing 747 has an economic life of more than 20 years, so its purchase cost of $150–200 million in 1996 terms is amortised over a longer period. It is more than twice as fast and carries 10 times the number of passengers. Frequencies on many routes are daily, so outside the required rest, crews have little down time. The cost of maintaining a modern jet is considerably less than for aircraft of the L749 and L1049 era.

The operating crews are also smaller in the modern aircraft. Automation has replaced the navigator and voice communications the radio officer. The flight engineer was the last to go, but eventually computer management of systems allowed the pilots to carry out this task as well. Duty periods are now shorter but relief pilots are still carried and proper rest areas are available for them in flight. (The L749 crews had to use regular seats in the cabin, while working and sleeping in a much noisier environment.)

THE 10,000-MILE FACTOR

Remoteness was a fact of life that Qantas engineers had learned to live with; they called it 'the 10,000-mile factor'. The introduction of the Constellation brought a new level of complexity to this old bugbear.

The L749s, like the Short flying boats, introduced many new technologies to flying. Yet the Qantas maintenance base, which had shifted to Mascot in Sydney with the move to land planes, was the proverbial 10,000 miles (about 16,000 kilometres) from sources of spares and expertise in either Britain or on the east coast of the United States, where the new and troublesome Wright Cyclone engines came from.

Down the years the 10,000-mile factor forced Qantas to become self-contained in every skill needed to maintain and modify its aircraft and

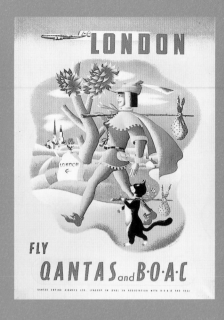

ABOVE: Qantas believed in bright posters to promote ticket sales. BELOW: In the London winter, pictures of Bondi Beach in summer would draw a crowd to the old Qantas offices in Bond Street.

engines and to build or sometimes invent the rigs and test equipment that it needed in order to keep them flying. The Kangaroo Route, covering nearly 12,000 miles from Sydney to London, also demanded advanced management of spares, not only in Sydney but in the engineering stations along the way. Some of these stations had Qantas staff but at others BOAC engineers were required to service what—for them, too—was a new aircraft.

ABOVE: Qantas Engine and Instrument Overhaul workshops, Vickers Avenue, Mascot. Established 1939, enlarged 1949, photographed 1950.

The Constellation's new features included an advanced automatic pilot, gyroscopic compass, and power assistance for the controls. In 1938 Qantas had established its own instrument repair shops in Sydney for the Short flying boats systems and had gained experience of increasingly complex American gear through the airline's work on wartime maintenance. But the Constellation's flight controls were the first to be power-assisted, which, while lightening the task considerably for the pilots, required duplicated hydraulic systems, backed up by electrical pumps. The system was something of a challenge for the maintenance teams.

The Constellation also introduced pressurisation to the Qantas fleet, allowing the crew and passengers to fly in comfort and higher altitudes— between 15,000 and 18,000 feet (about 4,500 to 5,450 metres)—where it was hoped that the weather would be better and the flight smoother.

Qantas assessed maintenance of the pressurisation system as essential for its operations. But Bendix, the American supplier, was not accustomed to dealing with airlines that wanted to do their own work. The American practice was to ship the unit to Bendix, which repaired and returned it. This suited airlines that were close to the Bendix facility, but not Qantas. Having looked at the way the pressurisation units were maintained, repaired and tested, Qantas engineers made up their own rigs in the Sydney workshops and proceeded to do all the work themselves.

The detailed knowledge of the system paid off for Qantas. Other operators spent years getting the Constellation's cabin environmental systems to work consistently. Qantas learned the hard way—from the basics up—to manage the systems to the extent where passengers, some of whom were executives of rival airlines, praised the maintenance of cabin comfort.

Before Qantas bought the Constellation, two incidents highlighted the stresses that pressurisation could cause. In one, a navigator was taking a sight through the astrodome of a TWA flight across the Atlantic when the perspex dome popped out. Tragically, the navigator was sucked out and lost. After this, all navigators were required to wear a harness while taking sights.

The other incident occurred on a domestic flight in the United States. The ground crews had failed to replace properly the cap to the toilet drain after emptying it on a turnaround. The cap blew off and an unfortunate passenger became a human plug as cabin pressure above and low pressure

below pinned her to the toilet seat. The crew had to de-pressurise the aircraft to release her, then make an emergency landing.

The biggest maintenance challenge came in the form of

ABOVE: Qantas menu for New Year's Day 1949.
BELOW: A 1940s cabin bag.

SPORTS RESULTS 1947–56

WIMBLEDON MEN'S SINGLES

Year	Winner	Runner-up	Score
1947	J A Kramer (1)	T P Brown (3)	6-1, 6-3, 6-2
1948	R Falkenburg (7)	J E Bromwich (2)	7-5, 0-6, 6-2, 3-6, 7-5
1949	F R Schroeder (1)	J Drobny (6)	3-6, 6-0, 6-3, 4-6, 6-4
1950	J E Patty (5)	F A Sedgman (1)	6-1, 8-10, 6-2, 6-3
1951	R Savitt (6)	K B McGregor (7)	6-4, 6-4, 6-4
1952	F A Sedgman (1)	J Drobny (2)	4-6, 6-2, 6-3, 6-2
1953	E V Seixas (2)	K Nielsen (U)	9-7, 6-3, 6-4
1954	J Drobny (11)	K R Rosewall (3)	13-11, 4-6, 6-2, 9-7
1955	M A Trabert (1)	K Nielsen (U)	6-3, 7-5, 6-1
1956	L A Hoad (1)	K R Rosewall (2)	6-2, 4-6, 7-5, 6-4

ENGLISH DERBY

Year	Winner	Jockey
1947	Pearl Diver	G Bridgland
1948	My Love	R Johnstone
1949	Nimbus	C Elliot
1950	Galcador	R Johnstone
1951	Arctic Prince	C Spares
1952	Tulyar	C Smirke
1953	Pinza	G Richards
1954	Never Say Die	L Piggott
1955	Phil Drake	F Palmer
1956	Lavandin	R Johnstone

MELBOURNE CUP

Year	Winner	Jockey
1947	Hiraji	J Purtell
1948	Rimfire	R Neville
1949	Foxzami	W Fellows
1950	Comic Court	P Glennon
1951	Delta	N Sellwood
1952	Dalray	W Williamson
1953	Wodalla	J Purtell
1954	Rising Fast	J Purtell
1955	Toparoa	N Sellwood
1956	Evening Peal	G Podmore

RUGBY UNION SERIES RECORDS - ENGLAND V AUSTRALIA

Year	Venue	Winners	Score
1948	Twickenham	Australia 1	11-0

TEST CRICKET RECORDS - ENGLAND V AUSTRALIA

Season	Tests	England	Australia	Draw	Ashes Held By
1946-47	5	0	3	2	Australia
1948	5	0	4	1	Australia
1950-51	5	1	4	0	Australia
1953	5	1	0	4	England
1954-55	5	3	1	1	England
1956	5	2	1	2	England

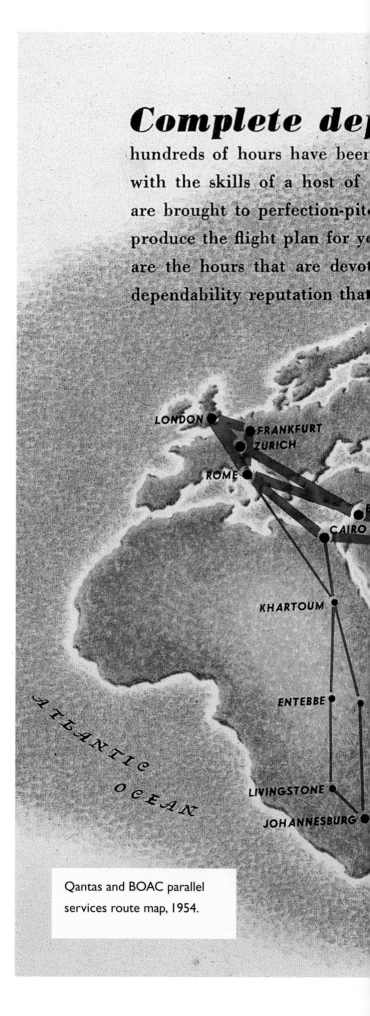

Complete dep

hundreds of hours have beer
with the skills of a host of
are brought to perfection-pit
produce the flight plan for y
are the hours that are devo
dependability reputation that

Qantas and BOAC parallel
services route map, 1954.

dability calls for many factors in airline operation. That's why to your journey already. These are the hours that contribute, painstakingly, technicians, to the Qantas pattern of dependability. Mighty modern engines experience and ability of your flight captain and navigator are combined to ey. Meteorological reports are translated into terms of flying comfort. These ating, for you, the surest, most enjoyable way to travel and, for Qantas, a byword among air-travellers from all parts of the world.

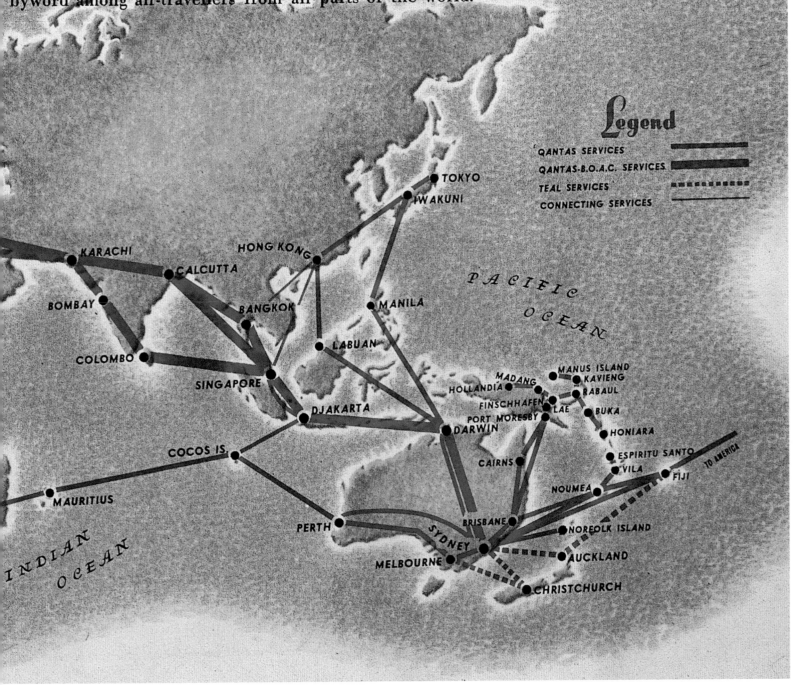

Legend

QANTAS SERVICES	
QANTAS-B.O.A.C. SERVICES	
TEAL SERVICES	
CONNECTING SERVICES	

the complex Constellation's Wright Cyclone 3000 hp engines.

In postwar aviation, piston engines were allowed only a limited life on the wing before they had to be removed, dismantled, checked, repaired, and completely rebuilt. Even so, they were prone to premature failures and between overhauls often needed expensive repairs, such as cylinder replacements and valves.

Even if all its systems were running properly, the complexity of the radial engine required continual attention, particularly the changing of spark plugs as required because of 'oiling' problems. Eventually Qantas discovered a way to resolve this situation. Before closing down for a refuelling halt, the engines were idled for two minutes.

When Qantas operated the Constellation and the Super Constellation, the airline found it necessary to position spare engines at most of the ports along the way. The Constellation was too confined to carry engines, so the airline used a Liberator, then converted one of its Lancastrians to become an engine-carrier.

A flight engineer constantly monitored the engines during flight. If one had problems, he would make a recommendation to the captain as to whether he should close it down. The captain had to make a decision, often in less than a minute, whether to return, divert or continue to the destination port. He had to take into account many factors. These could include the state of the engine, the likely problem and, if he decided to divert, whether a spare engine or parts would be available or whether the airline could find emergency accommodation for a plane load of passengers.

OPPOSITE: Four Wright Cyclone engines powered the Qantas Constellation. The Wright Cyclone (C 18 BDI) had a maximum power of 2,500 horsepower.

FLYING THE ROUTE

CHAPTER FOUR

For the pilots, the Lockheed 749 Constellation marked a huge step forward.

For the pilots, the Lockheed 749 Constellation marked a huge step forward. But, in some respects, flying the Constellation on the world's longest scheduled air route 50 years ago called on navigation skills and technologies that Captain James Cook would have found familiar on the *Endeavour* in 1769–70. In many parts of the world in the late 1940s, the network of aids and services that pilots now depend on had not been established. Once they left the support of major cities, such as London, Rome, Singapore or Sydney, the Constellation crews were virtually on their own, their only connection to the air traffic system the dots and dashes of hand-transmitted Morse and the ears of the radio operators, trained to detect incoming messages.

Today's Qantas pilot, who flies a Boeing 747–400 or a Boeing 767, would find the front office of the Constellation familiar but more complicated. The Constellation, as with all aircraft of its generation, used separate analogue instruments for every function that required monitoring. A pilot's scan took in instruments that showed direction, speed, altitude, whether the aircraft was climbing or descending, the rate of ascent or descent, its attitude and voice radio settings, as well as alarms and basic engine instruments. Today most of this information displays on video screens—either as required, or automatically if something is happening that needs attention.

In the Constellations, the throttles and propeller pitch controls, as well as the automatic pilot, were grouped between the pilots. There was a jump seat behind them for a third pilot during take-offs and landings, and on the starboard side the engineering console. Here the flight engineer monitored every aspect of engine performance and aircraft systems, such

ABOVE: A poster introducing the Constellation, produced in 1947.
OPPOSITE PAGE: Arrival of the first Qantas Constellation, *Ross Smith*, at Kingsford Smith Airport, Sydney. *Left to right:* The Minister for Civil Aviation, Mr Drakeford, Hudson Fysh (chairman and managing director of Qantas Empire Airways) and Sir Keith Smith.

as the electrical supply and the cabin environment. The engineer also controlled the engine-start buttons and had his own set of throttles and mixture controls. He used these to adjust individual throttle levers to synchronise the propellers and ensure the most efficient engine settings.

ABOVE: Radio officer Bill Taylor aboard Constellation VH-EAB *Lawrence Hargrave.*

The radio officer's position was on the opposite side of the aircraft. The Constellation had limited voice communications. Near airports, the pilot could talk on VHF (very high frequency) radio but only within visual range. Over the oceans and the lightly populated land masses, communication was by high frequency radio and Morse code. Every half hour, the operator had to tap out a position report. He also sent weather reports and noted, when required, incoming weather reports—for instance, forecasts for the destination of the flight sector. As part of international covenants, the radio operator had to maintain a watch on emergency frequencies. The operator would send messages called radiograms for passengers via commercial radio stations, which would relay the messages to their final destinations.

The radio operators had to keep their headphones on in all conditions. In stormy weather, they would often be trying to monitor a faint Morse signal with the volume turned up when a lightning flash would generate deafening static. In monsoon fronts, static from the lightning could be continuous, drowning out all signals as the operator strained to listen. Notwithstanding the difficulties, the radio operators played a vital role in this developmental phase of commercial aviation.

The navigator's 'office' was in a separate space behind a bulkhead. From today's perspective, the 'Vascos' (after the 15th-century Portuguese navigator and sailor Vasco da Gama) were the largely unsung heroes of the success of Qantas on long-distance routes. Because the airline flew over lonely, featureless oceans and land areas with no radio aids, the navigators depended on the sun, the moon, the planets and the stars. From the late 1930s through the 1950s and on into the jet age, Qantas assembled an outstanding team of celestial navigators.

During daylight and clear visibility, the crew could determine their position with landmarks—for instance, familiar islands while flying over Indonesia—which provided an accurate 'fix'. But from the moment the Constellations crossed the Great Dividing Range, the monotonous Australian outback rolled beneath the aircraft, with few towns, roads or railways to recognise. So the sextants were used as soon as the radio signals faded.

The navigator used a periscope sextant. At night he would look for stars, preferably spaced about 120 degrees apart. With the sextant he would read their angles in relation to an artificial horizon, then take the readings down to check them against tables. The readings should plot as a 'cocked hat', a small triangle within which would be the aircraft's position. Given good readings, a navigator would be accurate within five nautical miles (about nine kilometres).

During the day, he would take a sun sight or use the moon or one of the planets, such as Venus, if visible. From these readings, the navigator would check the position against the planned course and give the captain any corrections that were necessary.

ABOVE: Constellation flight engineer's instrument panels.
BELOW: Sextant used for navigation on the L749 Constellation.

RICHIE BENAUD

Benaud's pre-eminent qualities as a leading Nine Network and BBC commentator grew from his Test cricket career. He was the first Test player to make 2,000 runs and take 200 wickets in the period 1951–64. All this plus the Australian captaincy in 27 Tests (only four defeats).

'Qantas has been part of my cricketing and commentating life because in the early days of cricket touring we always went by ship to England. Then, suddenly in 1955, because of draconian government currency restrictions, we flew to the Caribbean for the series against the West Indies calling in at Tahiti, Mexico, Vancouver, Calgary (in a fierce snowstorm in what I recall as a DC3), Regina, Winnipeg, Toronto, Bahamas, Montego Bay and then Jamaica. It only took 52 hours!

'Then, in 1956, the year television began in Australia, it was Qantas from Calcutta to Sydney after the tour of India and Pakistan; in 1957/58 it was Sydney to Johannesburg in a Super Constellation via Cocos and Mauritius and in 1959/60 we ushered in the cricketing jet era with a Qantas Boeing 707–138 from Calcutta to Sydney, one of four such services a week.

'We weren't quite pioneers but it was very good to have Qantas looking after us in those early days.'

When neither the skies nor the ground were visible, the navigator would plot dead reckoning (DR) by making allowance for the push of any forecast winds on aircraft speed or heading, and take the first opportunity to confirm the DR position when he could make a sight. Although, in the absence of ground aids, the navigator would pick up commercial radio stations and plot their signals with a direction finder, transmissions could distort, particularly at dawn or dusk, and this method could be inaccurate.

During the Constellation (and Super Constellation) days, an aircraft routing would take into account the likelihood of engine failure. Qantas maintained current landing charts for all alternative airports in a special bag which was retained on the aircraft. At all times, the navigator had to be ready to give a new course and distances to the diversionary airport. The flight engineer would also be ready with information about fuel requirements, which would involve a special calculation for completing the journey on three engines.

From the navigator's point of view, as the journey progressed, the possibility of, and the need for, diversionary options would decline. After the Constellation flight had departed a main base, such as Sydney, which had spare engines and engineering strength, a return to Mascot might be more attractive than flying on to Darwin or diverting to some intermediate point which lacked full support. Similarly, if the weather was holding, continuing to London was probably preferable to returning to Tripoli in Libya. But with three engines, the flight might not be able to climb high enough to get over obstacles such as the Alps, so choices were always complicated.

To the modern passenger, this sounds a little frightening. But such procedures remain at the very heart of the Qantas tradition of safe operations. They began when Qantas flew single-engine aircraft in western Queensland, where engine failure left only one option: coming down. Then the operations manual carefully laid down the routes that should be followed and the alternative 'alighting areas' that were within gliding distance of the prescribed route.

ABOVE: Houses of Parliament, London. The city became a popular rest port for crews.

During each flight, crews logged any problems or malfunctions and, given the temperamental engines and systems, there was always something to note. At each stop, the first person on board was the station ground engineer who would ask the flight engineer for 'the book'. While cleaners tidied up the cabin and caterers loaded the galley for the next sector, the ground engineers worked flat out, invariably changing spark plugs and sometimes even cylinders. The two hours or so on the ground were like the pit stop in a Grand Prix.

The gardens of the Heliopolis Palace Hotel, Egypt, in the 1940s. OPPOSITE PAGE: The main interior salon of the hotel.

W hen the Constellation was introduced, the crew duty
period was 24 hours, which the captain could extend to
30 if it were operationally necessary. The three pilots
had a roster to enable them to rest one at a time during the flight.

The Qantas L749 usually carried two flight engineers, who took it turn
about, but only one navigator and one radio officer. Pilots at this time
were required to have some navigational and radio skills and most Qantas
captains had licences in one or both capabilities. While the navigator or
the radio officer rested, a pilot would replace them. The Constellation flew
high enough to clear obstacles on its route from Sydney to London but
constant crew awareness of ground heights below them continued to be
monitored. The habit grew out of long duty spells in unpressurised
Skymasters and flying boats, when the cruising height of 6,000 feet
(about 1,800 metres) was lower than the height of some large volcanoes
just off track.

The duty spells on the Kangaroo Route took the operating crew from
Sydney to Singapore, with an intermediate stop at Darwin, then to
Karachi with a halt at Calcutta. At
Singapore the resting crews stayed in
hotels. In Karachi they used a BOAC
hostel on the edge of the airport, a
cinder-block building without air-
conditioning. The next 'leg' was to Cairo,
with a rest in the attractive Heliopolis
Palace Hotel, which offered an honorary
membership of the nearby sports club.
At one stage the stewards stayed in a

houseboat on the Nile. The last leg was to London, via Tripoli in Libya and later via Rome, which also became a rest port for crews. In Britain, the crews stayed in Dormy House, the comfortable BOAC hostel (near the Sunningdale golf links) some 50 kilometres to the west of Heathrow Airport. In the very cold winters of 1947 and 1948, a time of shortages in Britain, the hostel could be freezing for crews fresh out of the Australian summer and the tropics of Singapore and Karachi. There was strict segregation at Dormy House: the women's quarters were across the road from the men's, linked by a tunnel.

As more flights were scheduled, the crews would be rested en route. They became familiar with Singapore. Crews on low Australian wages found this city expensive and while they stayed in quality hotels such as the Seaview, just out of town, they searched out Chinese restaurants where they could eat well at lower prices.

The Colosseum (above) became a familiar sight for passengers and crew when Rome was included as a stopover on the Kangaroo Route in October 1948.

In Karachi, Speedbird House (the local BOAC office) had been converted from wartime air force officers' accommodation, and was where the Australian flight and cabin crews, staying with British and other Australian colleagues, could let their hair down. There was plenty of tennis and swimming, and the occasional party.

As with Cairo, after a visit to the pyramids or a trip on the Nile, experienced crews found little to do in Karachi, except for souvenir buying in the bazaars. A typical 'slip' was two days, occasionally three. The first and last parts were spent sleeping after and before long duty hours.

A LONDON BASE

The range of the Constellation allowed Qantas to select routes that provided secure transits. The aircraft's operational flexibility also allowed Qantas to alter its route to take advantage of traffic preferences. In October 1948 Qantas increased the Kangaroo Route service from three flights per fortnight to two per week, again with passenger night-stops at Singapore and Karachi westbound and Cairo and Singapore eastbound. The following month the route shifted north from Tripoli to Rome.

The crew transfers were at Singapore, Karachi and Cairo and, at a later stage, in Rome. In this early period, Qantas was also to start basing crews in London, a policy it retained until well into the 1970s.

Flying between Sydney and London, or halfway around the world, the Qantas crews ran the full gamut of weather and flying conditions. When it was high summer in Australia, it was deep winter in Europe. Londoners still burned coal and 'pea-souper' fogs were still a characteristic of British life. Arrival time in London was scheduled for midday to early afternoon, which was the best time of the day. While there were some delays and diversions, the Constellations esta-blished a good operational record and, despite some engine and other problems, were able to maintain their timetable to a credible extent.

Another weather obstacle was what was then known as the 'inter-tropic front'. The heat from the sun is the engine that drives the fearsome weather patterns of the monsoon and its counter, the trade winds. The sun's apparent movement from north to south and back again

ABOVE: A visit to the Pyramids was a popular pastime for crews resting in Cairo.
BELOW: London's pea-souper fogs were a characteristic of British life until the 1950s.

over the earth's surface (which causes the seasons) gives rise to what is called 'the heat equator'—the area of the earth's surface in the tropics that appears to be directly under the sun and consequently warms up the most.

The monsoon front follows the heat equator. The break between the two weather systems is always marked somewhere by storms and high cloud. To the aviator, the front can look like the ramparts of a mighty castle, stretching up to an incredible 60,000 feet (about 18,000 metres). The huge cumulo-nimbus clouds flatten out at the top into an anvil shape, which designates them as fearsome thunderstorms.

ABOVE: Unpressurised aircraft had to thread their way through thunderstorms as best they could, flying below or through the disturbances.

Pilots can detect these storms from hundreds of miles away as the lightning fills the air with radio static. As the plane approaches, ominously black clouds can be seen, sometimes blue-black during the day and flickering with lightning. At night the lightning can look like a continuous artillery bombardment, stretching as far as the eye can see.

Unpressurised aircraft have to thread their way through these storms as best they can, flying below or through the disturbances. Jets, which cruise at 35,000 feet (10,600 metres) or higher, can see the tops, steer round them and use their radar to probe the course ahead.

The Constellations didn't have weather radar (it was introduced in the Super Constellations in the late 1950s) and had to penetrate the fronts using the eyes and skills of the pilots. Pressurisation, which was such an asset for 'normal' flying over temperate regions such as the United States and Europe, did not help much when aircraft had to penetrate the worst of these tropical fronts. Altitudes of 15,000–18,000 feet (4,500–5,500 metres) meant the aircraft had to fly through the middle of the cloud ramparts.

GREAT BALLS OF FIRE

Frequently, electrical potential built up in the aircraft and discharged along the wings and through the propellers in a blinding glow known as 'St Elmo's fire'. Sometimes a blue spear of fire would stretch out from the nose for some distance, then suddenly explode. The crews became familiar with the phenomenon, if not accustomed to it, and learned to look away before it exploded with a brilliant flash that would destroy night vision. There were several reports of fireballs inside aircraft.

One of these frightened both crew and passengers one night over India. The familiar electrical tension began to build up. As the glow started there was a sharp explosion in the cockpit and bright discharges boiled just behind the two startled pilots. Suddenly this turned into a fireball and rolled out of the flight deck and along the corridor into the passenger cabin. Passengers were screaming when it exploded and disappeared. No one was hurt and there was no damage. Stiff drinks all round were the order of the night.

While flying the Kangaroo Route in the early days was fun, it was also hard work, a meticulous team effort under conditions that would now be regarded as primitive. It was work that laid the foundation for the huge Qantas expansion through the 1950s, '60s and '70s, built the Qantas tradition for safety and reliability, and produced the modern airline that we now know.

ABOVE: Representatives of three airlines which joined hands in a new Commonwealth air partnership in 1960. *Left to right:* Pat Eppy, of Earls Court, a BOAC receptionist; Meena Mudnani, of Bombay, of Air India International; and Jean Fraser, of Wembley, who was a receptionist with Australia's Qantas Empire Airways. They were photographed in London.

CHAPTER FIVE

IN-FLIGHT SERVICE

As the Constellation ushered in a new, five-star era, the stewards—who had not yet been joined by hostesses—were kept busy.

As the Constellation ushered in a new, five-star era, the stewards— who had not yet been joined by hostesses—were kept busy. Initially there were three of them. They had a galley with ovens and refrigeration to look after 38 passengers and a flight crew of seven. They also had a full bar, fine crockery and linen. A Qantas flight kitchen, first at Rose Bay in Sydney and then at St Marys, prepared and froze food which was shipped to stations along the way and picked up where there was no suitable local caterer. The airline started the tradition of using an Australian motif on its menus. These opened to a first fold which grandiosely listed dishes with imposing French names; on the second fold was the English translation. The menus usually offered a salad and some starters, then a choice of fish, chicken or beef, prepared simply as a grill or a roast. Finally desserts, all presented with panache.

Qantas also carried Australian wines. After one trip, the Australian Minister for External Affairs, Richard (later Lord) Casey, grumpily chided the airline for not having an adequate French cellar.

The aircraft were in the air for sectors of 10 hours or even more. While they still made overnight stops, at least in the earlier days, in-flight service became an essential ingredient of the Qantas product and a feature on which it built its fine reputation.

When the airline slid into war with the rest of the world, many stewards had become loadmasters and pursers. Some joined the services. Others returned to the merchant marine and worked on troopships. By the end of World War II, cabin service personnel in Qantas had dwindled to three catering staff and five flight stewards. The first priority was to recruit more, if nothing else to replace Bill Drury, who left Qantas in 1945. In 1946, when recruitment was in full swing, there were 14 flight

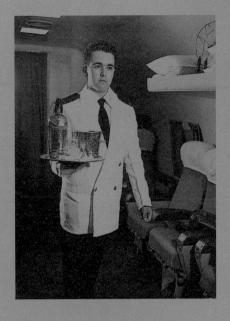

ABOVE: Silver service on a Super Constellation.
BELOW: First Qantas winter uniforms, 1948 to late 1952.
OPPOSITE PAGE: One of the original nine Qantas hostesses, Patricia Bourke, on service in 1948.

JOHN NEWCOMBE

As a singles player, Newcombe's victories included three Wimbledon titles and, with Tony Roche, five Wimbledon doubles championships. His success on court has been matched by his off-court success as a businessman and Davis Cup captain.

'My first trip overseas was in December 1960 as a 16-year-old when I flew from Sydney to Miami to represent Australia in Junior Davis Cup competition. In March 1961 I left Australian shores again on a seven-month tour as part of the four-man Australian men's team. On each of those occasions I went through a period of feeling homesick and one of my greatest joys was stepping on to the Qantas plane that was bound home to Australia.

'Apart from the Qantas safety record that is second to none, I honestly believe Qantas is as good as any airline in the world, and better than most. I am proud to be an Australian and proud to recognise Qantas and their 50 years of outstanding service on the Kangaroo Route.'

stewards. The numbers increased as the Hythe flying boats and the Lancastrians developed the services to London. But the Qantas service identity started in 1947, coinciding with the introduction of the Lockheed 749 Constellations.

On the first Constellation flights, the cabin crew quickly struck up a rapport with the passengers because they flew all the way to London, sharing some of the same night-stops. Qantas used the aircraft's cargo space to carry supplies as required.

HIGH PRAISE

London magazine executive Charles Sims was an early passenger from London to Sydney on the Constellation service. He marvelled that he could fly to Sydney, spend six days there and be back in London in 13 days. Among the 38 passengers on his flight, he recorded, there were three 'distinguished scientists', a brigadier, several other army officers, businessmen and seven small children from one to four years of age and their mothers, who were joining their husbands in either Singapore or Australia.

An experienced flier, Sims had scrutinised Qantas service. He noted that the 'skipper' came through the cabin on night stages at least twice, checking on the air-conditioning and the lighting.

'From what I saw [the stewards were] exceptional. How they coped with the babies on the way out left me bewildered. They were completely unconcerned if three babies were on the gangway floor when they were serving tea or lunch. I saw one with a tray of crockery in one hand retrieve a piece of a puzzle from underneath a seat with the other and cheerfully put it in its place...

'They look after everybody's little worries, take charge of baggage, hats or coats and serve tea at 3 o'clock in the morning as though it were a vicarage lawn on a Sunday afternoon... One feels that the service one gets is sincere and really friendly.'

BOAC's chairman Sir Miles Thomas had a keen eye for detail, and praised the Qantas service in a note he wrote to his staff in 1950:

'I have noticed a considerable difference between the Qantas 749 Constellations and the two BOAC Constellations in which I travelled out. The Qantas aircraft are properly air-conditioned and they seem to

IN-FLIGHT SERVICE

handle the cabin pressure rather better than we do, because at no time was the pressure inside the cabin greater than 4,000 feet altitude. My pocket altimeter told me … that BOAC aircraft were running at about 8,000 feet and that has a considerable effect on passengers' ears. In the Qantas Connies they have hot and cold water in the toilets whereas hot was conspicuously missing on BOAC machines … Qantas serve their food on china plates which hold the heat and are much more attractive than the plastic plates of BOAC.'

Not mentioned by Sir Miles in his diary notes were some of the little tricks that stewards could play.

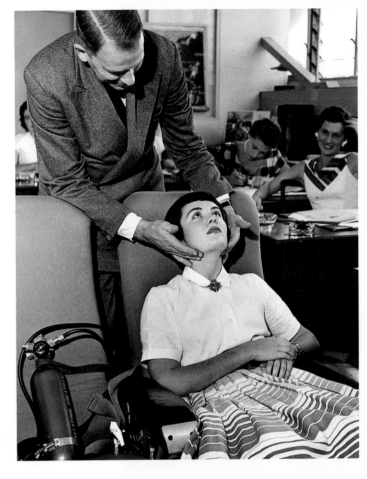

Qantas policy was quite firm: no tipping. The message was on the bottom of all the menus. The older and bolder stewards, from the ships, would produce a pair of scissors and clip off the no-tips statement. One chief steward had it down to a fine art. He was, in the words of his colleagues, 'a bit of a conjurer' and would rush up to the door as the passengers were leaving. As the first passenger went out, he would brush down the passenger's coat and say loudly: 'Thank you, sir!' A £5 note would magically appear between his fingers and be pushed into his jacket. The other passengers got the message.

Another old chief steward trick was in Economy service, when passengers had to pay for their drinks. After he had served a round of drinks, the gloved chief would pop a metal drinks tray into the oven. Any passengers who had paid in notes would get their change back on the hot tray. They would reach for the money and jerk their hands back. 'Thank you, sir!' the chief would bellow as he retreated back to the galley, with

ABOVE: Dr E H Anderson, Qantas Director of Medical Services, with a trainee hostess in the developmental era of international air travel.
OPPOSITE PAGE: The first Qantas hostesses. *Left to right:* Joy Bruce, Patricia Burke, Margaret Calf, Irma Wharton, Marj de Tracy, Joy Daniell, Adrienne Gundlinger, Ros Allison and Margaret Lamb. On the ground is Mike Furniss, senior instructor.

the coins still on the tray. These practices have long since been consigned to mere memories of the 'good old days'.

Unlike today's aircraft, the Constellations were divided into three cabins. Passengers in the same section would develop friendships during the long flights. One regular traveller produced a Scrabble board when the game was new and quickly drew a coterie who played almost non-stop for the rest of the journey. If VIPs were flying, the crew could seat them in a compartment more or less separate from the rest of the passengers.

ABOVE: The aircraft captain points out scenic items of interest to tourist passengers in a Super Constellation c. 1954.

On later Constellations, there were bunks in the rear of the aircraft which passengers could book. Sometimes, however, these were reserved for invalids or wounded soldiers returning home.

On the first flights, some passengers complained that the seats were too close together and it was difficult to sleep. *'The seats themselves are comfortable but when they are pushed back you find little leg room,'* one reported. Later Qantas was able to make better use of the difficult, circular cabin for passenger comfort.

During the flight, the captain would regularly distribute reports to passengers giving the aircraft's location, speed and the estimated time to the next stop. On the Kangaroo Route, remaining on board at some stops was often preferable to disembarking to stretch the legs. Calcutta terminal had a reputation for being crowded and noisy. The arrival in Darwin was a similarly dismal occasion. *'We were kept waiting for what seemed a very long time for the immigration, health and other formalities to be completed in a small, very hot room,'* a British passenger complained. *'The mothers of small children became increasingly concerned after an hour had gone by and nothing had been done.'*

Another passenger wrote this diatribe about Cairo: *'We were all requested to keep our seats and in due course a comic gentleman appeared with a Flit gun. He sprayed the inside of the aircraft with some vile-smelling liquid then slammed the door on us, leaving us there for five to 10 minutes.*

'The immigration, health and customs shed is the really silly part. It is very small and crowded with passengers from three or four flights endeavouring to obtain their pass from a number of querulous clerks arguing with each other.

'The episode was made all the more fantastic because someone had placed a complete motorcycle and sidecar just inside the entrance, to the annoyance of everyone including the police. But no one had the idea of moving it.'

Some of the passengers wrote about the sheer joy of flying. The Cairo complainer, a photographer, wrote that all the way from London the visibility was uncharacteristically clear and from 17,500 feet (about 5,400 metres) he enjoyed the views over Paris, Lake Geneva, the Alps (*'Matterhorn on the left, Mount Blanc on the right'*) and Italy.

At night-stops, the passengers and crew went to their overnight lodgings and were wakened early the next morning for the departure.

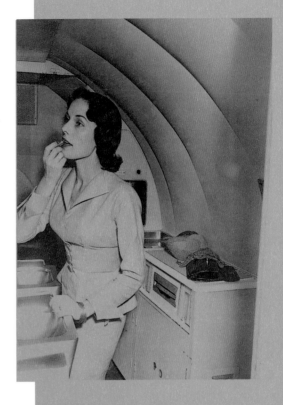

ABOVE: A passenger freshens up in one of the spacious rest rooms at the back of the Super Constellation.

WHEN THE WOMEN JOINED

Until the Constellation services, Qantas cabin service had been in the hands of stewards. The Australian domestic airlines, ANA and the relatively new TAA had employed hostesses only to crew their cabins, as did the American airlines. Qantas saw the need to employ women when it began the Constellation flights at the end of 1947.

ABOVE: Hostesses and stewards anticipated passengers' wishes on early international flights.

More women began to travel. Senior diplomats, public servants, government ministers, members of parliament and businessmen were increasingly accompanied by their wives when they flew to overseas engagements or on postings. Through the 1950s the British maintained substantial forces in Singapore and Malaya (as it was then) and wives of senior officers were spared the discomfort of the traditional troop ship and allowed to fly to their postings and home on leave. Also, more children flew from schools in England or Australia to spend the holidays in Singapore with their parents before returning to school for the new term.

Qantas decided that, like the domestic airlines and its Pacific cousin, British Commonwealth Pacific Airlines, it needed women staff on its flights to service the female and juvenile component of its patronage. In many ways, they were truly hostesses, making sure their passengers were safe and comfortable, and attending to the needs of mothers and children.

W hen Qantas announced that it would recruit women, it received more than 1,000 applications, and those shortlisted underwent a rigorous interview program. The selection panel of Mrs Hudson (later Lady) Fysh, staff executive Bruce Hinchcliffe, traffic manager Bill Nielson and general manager George Harman chose the initial nine. Marj de Tracy, who had flight hostess experience, was recruited as supervisor. The recruits came from ANA, TAA and BCPA.

In the next intake, two were girls who had worked in the Qantas head office. The applicants had to be about

LEFT: Hostesses took care of unaccompanied children.

The Qantas attention to service and style helped to establish its reputation as a leader in the field of international air travel.

1.7 metres tall, weigh about 60.5 kilograms, have first-aid experience and preferably a nursing background, be well educated, have 'people' skills, preferably with a second language and some experience in secretarial work. For all this they were to be paid £5 a week (in present day terms about $250), with a £2 weekly service allowance.

Marj de Tracy and traffic instructor Mike Furniss gave the new recruits a rapid course ranging over company history, the anatomy of the airline, a technical rundown on the Constellation and how to handle the in-flight paperwork. The girls flew a sector or two on various Qantas flights as passengers before they started service. The first Qantas flight with a working hostess aboard, Marj de Tracy, departed on 8 May 1948.

Hostesses reported to the captain and helped him with the paperwork.

The conservatively uniformed Qantas hostesses were taught how to handle aircraft and customs declarations and health certificates, to take care of immigration formalities on the many stops along the way, and to help passengers complete their forms. At that time red tape ruled when it came to international travel. Australians, for instance, had to get an income tax clearance before they left the country. Foreign currency was a mystery. Forms in foreign languages were beyond the comprehension of most.

The first Qantas hostesses were also lectured in minute detail on the unfamiliar world beyond their native shores. They copied into thick exercise books facts and figures not only about scheduled stops such as Singapore, Cairo and London but about places the aircraft might (and occasionally did) divert to, such as Bahrain. At Cairo, for instance, the hostesses had to gather all the crew certificates and passenger passports for an immigration check before passengers and crew were allowed to go to the beds, showers and hot meals that awaited them on their overnight stop at the Heliopolis Palace Hotel. In Singapore, anyone who wanted to see the sights would join their hostess at Raffles for a bus tour of what was then a war-battered British colony.

A night out? The hostess notes carried information for passengers about the Great World and Happy World amusement parks with their packed dance floors and expensive drinks, too costly then for the modestly paid Australian flight and cabin crews.

As the schedules changed, so did the last stopover before London. For a while both passengers and crew stayed over at Cairo, then crews began to 'slip' at Rome. The London stopover could be for a few days and the crew got a seven-day break there every few weeks.

While the hostess's life was glamorous, it was more often than not extremely hard work. The women were away for up to 35 days on every cycle. Two or three might share a flat in Sydney but were more likely to meet along the route. The eastbound and westbound hostesses, for instance, shared Room 66 at Raffles in Singapore and one girl was always arriving as the other was departing. Raffles had no air-conditioning and the windows opened onto the Palm Court, a dignified Singapore

BELOW: Passengers relax aboard a Constellation.

nightspot, where a band played on until the early hours while the exhausted hostesses tried to sleep.

En route, engine problems were frequent. One former hostess recalls an unscheduled landing at Basra, where no spare engine was available. The aircraft was on the ground for three days and she did not get a night in bed for the whole time. As supervisor, Marj de Tracy required every hostess to report to her at Mascot the day after each flight to submit a written report detailing every incident that had occurred. A typical stay in Sydney could be eight days between trips, with four of these taken up in reports, training and briefings.

The experiences made for refinements of the Qantas style of service. For instance, in London, the local manager agreed to carry, unescorted, a little girl of three flying from her grandparents in Britain to her parents in New Zealand. *'The hostess will look after her,'* he said. A three-year-old requires almost constant attention and the duty hostesses on the long flight found that they could not combine the burden of an active child with their normal duties. On two stopovers, they had a cot made up in their room to look after the girl. Three hostesses detailed the problem on their return and Qantas eventually evolved a system whereby office staff were placed on a roster so they could volunteer to accompany 'a minor' if required. It wasn't a cheap solution. The Qantas attention to children quickly spread by word of mouth among travelling families, enhancing the reputation of Qantas for aware and friendly service.

Mixing hostesses with the young men of the flight crews (most of the captains and stewards were senior

men with families) was a recipe for romance. The peripatetic lifestyle made it difficult but not impossible for the younger first officers and engineers, many of whom were just out of wartime service, to get together with the hostesses.

Several of the first girls married flight crew. Lilian Heal and first officer Rod McAlpine repeatedly met along the route, mainly on the tennis court in places such as Karachi and back home in Neutral Bay, Sydney, where Lilian had a flat. They married in 1951. Queenslander Patricia Burke was in the same crew as Val St Leon, the chief flight engineer who later trained as a pilot and retired as a captain. When they landed in London he invited her to fly to Paris for dinner and proposed to her at a candle-lit table. When first officer Jim Carroll became ill in Karachi, Margaret McLachlan looked after him. *'I was determined not to become attached to flight crew, but my maternal instincts took over and we married,'* she says, 47 years later.

The aviation world was a small community in the Constellation days. Stewards and hostesses got to know regular travellers and were hailed as friends if they bumped into them on the streets in London or Sydney.

A decade later, the number of Qantas hostesses had grown to almost 100. By this time the job was even more glamorous and exciting. The Super Constellations were in service and Qantas flights were heading around the world. The Kangaroo Route westbound from Australia to London and Europe was the busiest. Every week two of the Southern Cross flights, eastbound over Honolulu to San Francisco, continued to New York and London. The hostesses, stewards and flight crews had more

BELOW: Hostess in winter uniform in the late 1940s.

generous rosters that gave them stopovers in these exciting places. There were more flights per week, so opportunities for manipulating rosters—to enjoy, say, a week in New York or to begin holiday leave in London—could be arranged. The pay (by then about £10 a week) was still by no means generous. But flight allowances were improved greatly so that crew were not necessarily out of pocket for meals and other expenses while they were away.

Shortly after the Constellation service started, Prime Minister Ben Chifley travelled to London for a Prime Ministers' conference. One of the first hostesses, Pat Burke (as she was then), recalls fetching him his hat on arrival as he prepared to review a Royal Air Force guard of honour. *'It's the 'at with the 'ole,'* Chifley said.

It was a time in which, staff recall, passengers were not only an elite but dressed that way. For men, a three-piece suit and a hat were essential. For women, hat and gloves were de rigueur, as if attending a garden party rather than preparing for the ordeal of hours in the air. The formalities dominated when Prime Minister Robert Menzies took to the air for his first visit to Britain after his 1949 election.

Margaret Carter, a flight hostess on both the Super Constellations and later on 707s, says of those years: *'Flight hostessing for young, adventurous women was a very sought-after position.'* Proud to speak for her select generation of hostesses, she adds: *'It was a privilege to represent Australia on Qantas and at the same time see the world.'*

BELOW: Margaret Carter joined Qantas as a flight hostess in 1958.

SUPER CONSTELLATION DAYS

CHAPTER SIX

By 1954 the Super Constellation had progressively replaced the Lockheed 749 Constellation...

By 1954 the Super Constellation had progressively replaced the Lockheed 749 Constellation. The intervening six years had seen great change for Qantas, Australia and the world. Europe was struggling out of the threat of another war as the Berlin airlift foiled the Russian blockade. India and Pakistan were enjoying their first years of independence. Japan's economy was reborn, sparking that country's emergence as an important trading partner for Australia. At the beginning of the period the schoolroom maps still showed the British Empire as large splotches of pink. At the end, only patches remained. Of these, Malaya and Singapore were still colonies but were self-ruling and on the way to independence.

There were similar dynamics in the aviation industry, which had been transformed by World War II. Huge leaps were made in the technology of aircraft; air forces moved quickly from piston-engined aircraft to jets or turbo-props; and there were advances in radio, navigation and landing aids, air traffic control and aircraft control systems.

Perhaps most important was the development of aviation infra-structure. Led by the United States, the Allied Forces created sealed airfields all over the world, with long runways capable of launching heavy bombers. Before the war, flying boats seemed the way to the future because the big, multi-engined aircraft could take off and land almost anywhere. However, as the Qantas experience had demonstrated, flying boats were difficult to maintain and expensive to operate, and could be lost in landing accidents, even in sheltered waters—for instance, by holing the hull on a half-submerged log.

In 1947 Australia had just launched its postwar migration program, which was to expand the population from between seven and eight million

ABOVE: The galley in a L1049G Super Constellation .
BELOW: Opening new sightseeing vistas for passengers, the Super Constellation windows were rectangular instead of round and enlarged to 16 by 18 inches to give each an 85 per cent increase in visibility over earlier models.
OPPOSITE PAGE: A Super Constellation.

1957–66

WORLD EVENTS

• Cosmonaut Yuri Gagarin of the Soviet Union became the first man to complete a successful space flight on 12 April 1961.

• President John F Kennedy was assassinated in Dallas, Texas, on 22 November 1963.

• The Australian Government announced on 29 April 1965 commitment of an 800-strong infantry battalion to Vietnam, reinforcing its advisers already serving with American units.

SPORTS

• Australia's Jack Brabham won his second world Formula One motor racing championship on 29 August 1960 driving a Cooper.

• Rod Laver was the first Australian to win the tennis Grand Slam with victories in the Australian, Wimbledon, French and United States Singles championships in 1962.

• Australian Dawn Fraser became the first female swimmer to win a 100-metre freestyle gold medal in three successive Olympics (Melbourne 1956, Rome 1960, and Tokyo in 1964).

• Donald Campbell broke the world landspeed record on Lake Eyre, South Australia, with 403.1 mph on 17 July 1964.

POP CULTURE

• *The Sundowners*, directed by Fred Zinnermann, starring Robert Mitchum and Deborah Kerr and based on Jon Cleary's novel, opened in New York on 11 December 1960.

• Crooner Frank Sinatra enraptured a packed Sydney Stadium audience with his performance on 30 November 1961.

• The Beatles topped the Sinatra-inspired hysteria when they toured Australia in 1964.

• Professor Afferbeck Lauder's study of the Australian language *Let's Talk Strine* became a bestseller in 1965. Professor Lauder, alias designer Alistair Morrison, began his research after novelist Monica Dickens was asked by a fan at a book launch 'How much is it?' and inscribed the book 'Emma Chissit'.

Super Constellation production at Lockheed in the 1950s. Assembly line scene shows five fuselages under construction in rear. As aircraft in the foreground moved down the line, those in the rear advanced to receive wings, engines and tail assemblies.

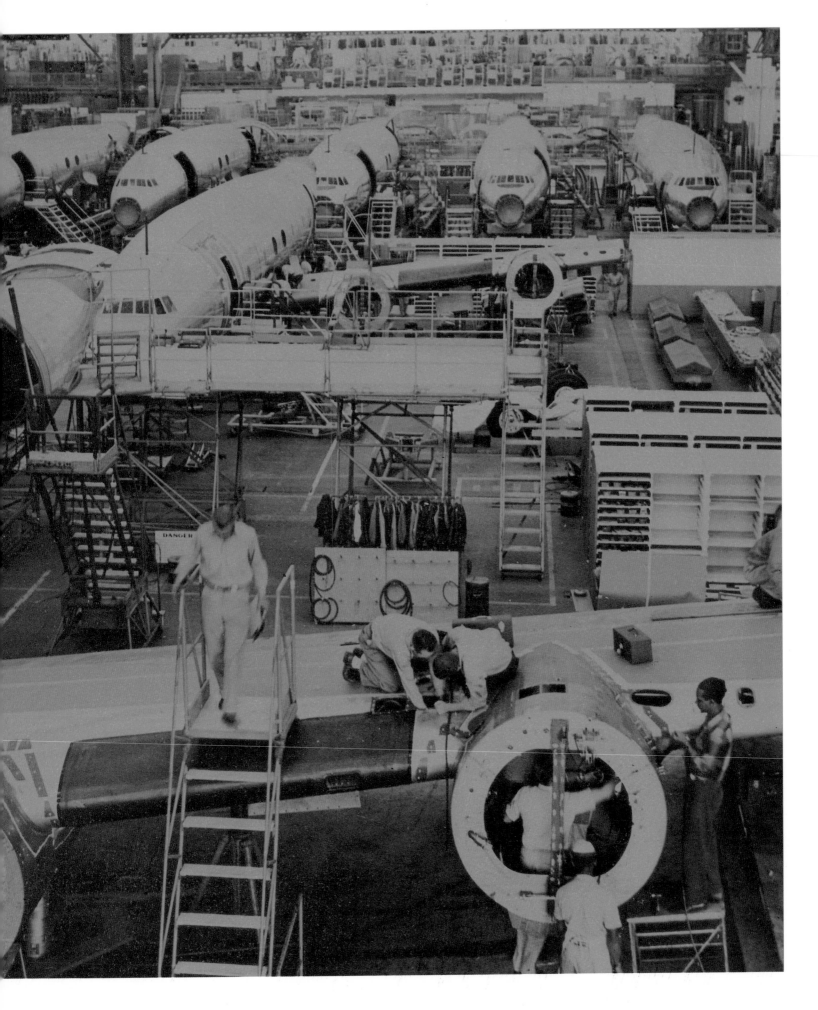

in the 1940s to 18 million by 1996–97 and build a multi-racial, multi-cultural society.

Politically, the climate in Australia was about to change. The Labor Government was replaced in 1949 by Prime Minister Robert (later Sir Robert) Menzies and a coalition of the Liberal and Country Parties. The Menzies era, which can be said to have lasted beyond that particular prime-ministership until 1972, was a period of solid economic prosperity for Australia. It saw huge growth in mining, the rural industries, manufacturing and commerce. In the early 1950s wool prices surged beyond the magic 'pound-a-pound' level, which, with good farming years, brought short-lived riches to the rural population.

It was a period in which the British aircraft industry was unable to deliver competitive aircraft on time—with the notable exception of the short-haul Vickers Viscount—even though Qantas had wanted to 'buy British', partly out of loyalty and partly because of dollar shortages.

Of the American manufacturers, the leaders were Lockheed and Douglas. The DC3 was the mainstay of short-haul air services in every country of the world. The DC4, with four-engines, was ubiquitous on the long-haul and over-water routes. Lockheed had to come from behind but, even with the Constellation and the Super Constellation, faced intense rivalry from the Douglas DC6 and DC7 families. All four were pressurised, fast and capable of making money for airlines. Boeing, with its early Stratoliner and later Stratocruiser, lagged well behind, even though its factories were busy with big bombers for the US Air Force, which was later to give the Seattle company a head start in the race into jets.

'For Qantas, the acquisition of Constellations was by far the single most important postwar decision; it was to become the central factor in

ABOVE: A poster featuring the Super Constellation, issued on the airline's 70th anniversary in 1990.
BELOW: A caricature of Hudson Fysh.

THE LONGEST HOP

growth and development of their operational and commercial expertise,' John Gunn wrote in *Challenging Horizons*, the second volume of his Qantas history. *'From the chaos of the war years and ad hoc operators that followed them, there began the rapid emergence of a great world airline with its route expansion across both the southern Indian Ocean to Africa and across the Pacific to America to make Qantas, within a decade, the first airline ever to operate a scheduled service circling the world.'*

LOCKHEED

Lockheed was good for Qantas and Australia. But for that matter Australia was, and is still, good for Lockheed.

Before World War II, Reginald Myles Ansett bought Lockheed 10 Electras for his fledgling airline, travelling the Victorian countryside, as Ginty McGinness had done for Qantas nearly two decades before in Queensland, selling shares in his start-up carrier. The Royal Australian Air Force operated Lockheed Hudsons and Venturas during the war. Qantas operated the L10 Electra and Lodestars during the war and on Queensland services and eventually bought six L749 Constellations and leased another. It operated 16 of the later, faster and bigger Super Constellations. Qantas, Ansett and TAA in the 1950s ordered the turbo-prop Lockheed Electras. The postwar RAAF bought first the Lockheed Neptune maritime patrol aircraft, then various models of the C130 Hercules transport (the latest the C130J in 1996) and the Lockheed Orion maritime patrol aircraft. Because they shared the same basic engines, Qantas was able to support the RAAF with engine overhauls for all these types.

ABOVE: Lady Spender, wife of Sir Percy Spender (Australian Ambassador to the United States) christening the first Super Constellation *Southern Constellation* on 29 March 1954.

Eventually Lockheed, without a competing aircraft, was to support Boeing in its successful bid for the Qantas order for jets in the late 1950s, with the two companies providing an advantageous trade-in offer that smoothed the airline's transition from piston-engined aircraft to jets.

From 1948, when the Constellations prevailed against the slower BOAC aircraft on the Kangaroo Route, the main challenge for Qantas was obtaining government approval to buy new aircraft. The Menzies Government was constrained, as the reluctant owner of Qantas, by the need for substantial amounts of new capital to finance such acquisitions. It was also under pressure to limit dollar spending. Even in the later years, when Qantas could demonstrate that trade-ins and deferred payments would cover Super Constellation purchases, the airline invariably had to go to Lockheed and seek extensions of option deadlines. Sometimes a panic-stricken government, facing an overdrawn dollar budget, demanded cancellation of an order; but somehow each crisis was surmounted and Qantas slowly built its fleet.

As Qantas operations on the Kangaroo Route grew, the airline sought to consolidate its position as

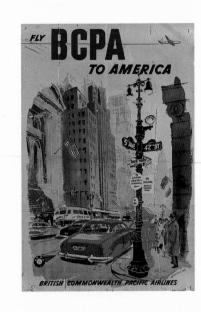

Australia's designated international carrier by opening new services to Hong Kong and Japan, eventually using Douglas DC4 Skymasters, and adding cities such as Jakarta and Colombo to its Kangaroo Route schedules. After a survey flight across the Indian Ocean in a Lancastrian, which indicated a need for an improved airstrip on the Cocos Islands, Qantas inaugurated its weekly Constellation service to South Africa, via Mauritius, in 1952. Although the route lost money, Qantas and the Australian Government saw it as providing an alternative to South-East Asia and the Middle East in the event of another war—a possibility which, in those troubled years, was far from remote.

Qantas planners strongly advocated an easterly route to Britain and Europe, via the United States, citing both strategic and commercial considerations. In an era when the concept of international carriers being operated by interested governments was seen as a potential force for peace, Australia, Britain and New Zealand established British Commonwealth Pacific Airlines (BCPA). By 1950 it had become apparent that it was a mistake to prop up BCPA, which lost both the Pacific marketing battle and money.

BELOW: Hudson Fysh speaking at the departure ceremony of the first regular Qantas service to South Africa on 1 September 1952.

In 1954 Qantas took over BCPA when it received its first L1049 Super Constellations. Even so, the L749 Constellations flew on in Qantas colours until October 1955. The last in service was the *Charles Kingsford Smith*, the Constellation that had made history by inaugurating the London route. Well operated and well maintained, the Qantas 749s retired gracefully as trade-ins, providing a substantial part of the financing for the new Super Constellations.

With its deft stewards and attentive hostesses, Qantas built a reputation for service and caring for passengers on the long flights of the Super Constellation era. The glamour of travel *(right)* was reflected in promotional displays.

BELOW: A 40th anniversary year menu which grandiosely listed dishes with imposing French names.

ITA BUTTROSE

Ita Buttrose's career has encompassed print, radio and television as well as community service. Former editor of *The Australian Women's Weekly* as well as publisher of all ACP magazines, she became Editor-in-Chief of News Limited's *Daily* and *Sunday Telegraphs*. She subsequently became editor of the *Sun Herald*. Ita currently runs her own national public relations consultancy.

'Qantas stirs the Australian in me. It makes me proud of my heritage and the remarkable history of this great airline. Qantas for me means Australia. The moment I step on board my Qantas plane after a spell overseas, I feel I'm home, even though I might have a 23-hour flight ahead of me! I love hearing the Australian accent again as we're welcomed aboard. When I take my seat I feel totally relaxed, secure in the knowledge that I'm flying on the world's safest airline. The Qantas flight crew is one who knows the importance of Simply Superior Customer Service, something I often speak about on the professional speaking circuit.

'I hope our mighty airline, which had such small beginnings, continues to prosper on its Kangaroo Route!'

BELOW: The sleek, elongated nose housed the weather radar on some of the Super Constellations.

SELECTIVE EXCELLENCE

The Super Constellation was about 5.3 metres longer than its predecessor, which accentuated the graceful sweep of the original design. The increased wingspan allowed extra tankage, which provided more range. The engines were a more powerful version of the Curtis Wright Cyclone, known as the turbo-compound, which gained extra power by milking the thrust previously lost in the exhaust gases. The aircraft would carry up to 80 passengers at about 528 kilometres per hour. Eventually it would acquire a longer nose to house a radar and wingtip tanks, both features enhancing the aircrafts' performance as well as its appearance.

To develop the L1049, Lockheed bought back from Howard Hughes the original Constellation and modified its fuselage and wings before beginning an extensive test program. Qantas engineers were keen followers of the development and saw it as the answer to the airline's capacity problems, at least in the mid-1950s. At first it seemed like only an interim choice, as both jets and turbo-props were on the design boards and promised far greater speeds than the piston-engined aircraft, as well as lower costs and much simpler maintenance.

At this time aircraft manufacturers were developing new designs at a rapid rate. In Britain, de Havilland had launched the Comet, the world's first jet passenger airliner, which made its pioneer test flight in 1949. The Comet was powered by de Havilland's Ghost engine, which even by the standards of the day was primitive. De Havilland proposed later versions with more powerful engines, but Qantas engineers were still doubtful about it. Later it became obvious that the American manufacturers, including Boeing, were also looking at jet airliners.

To keep up with these developments, Qantas posted engineers to the various manufacturers on the American west coast. Senior operations and engineering executives made frequent trips to the factories to keep themselves informed. In Sydney, analysts carefully tracked all the information and applied the data to specific Qantas requirements, such as traffic potential, routes and the limitations of airports. For Qantas it was critical to ensure that, when the time came to buy the next generation of aircraft, the best possible choice was made. For Qantas to survive in a competitive world against airlines that were bigger and stronger than it

ABOVE: Super Constellation propellers had a diameter of 15 feet.
BELOW: The wingtip tanks of the Super Constellation extended the range of the aircraft by some 650 miles, giving it a total range of 3,215 miles.

ABOVE: A caricature of C O Turner. BELOW: Turner demonstrates a model of a Super Constellation to Sir Percy Spender (Australian Minister to Washington) at a Los Angeles press conference.

was, it had to assess both costs and potential yields to ensure profitability. As Qantas had discovered as far back as the 1920s in Longreach, selecting the best possible aircraft was the key to its survival.

The proliferation of types which were optimistically promised from 1953 onwards made the airline's decision difficult on purely technical grounds. The situation was reflected within Qantas. On the commercial side, it would be difficult to offset any hardware investments that were less than cautious, as air fares were highly regulated by a combination of agreements through the International Air Transport Association (IATA) machinery, supported by the need for government approval of all fares.

Qantas was originally attracted by the L1049 Super Constellation as an aircraft that would take it as far as the mid-1950s. But the likely successors, such as turbo-props, were being developed much more slowly than the manufacturers' hype suggested. Eventually the cold logic of engineering analysis showed that models of the L1049 would see Qantas through to the introduction of jets in 1959–60.

The earlier promises of aircraft such as the Bristol Britannia and the de Havilland Comet either could not deliver on performance or encountered serious delays. The British introduced political pressures that were even heavier than the 1946 battle when the British Government had worked to head off Qantas from ordering the original L749 from Lockheed.

For Qantas, a further complication was the relationship with BOAC, its partner on the Kangaroo Route. The British Government poured millions of pounds into the aircraft industry. As owner of BOAC it required the airline to buy British equipment and to persuade Qantas to buy the Comet. The first objective was to head off any Super Constellation order, which the British feared would pre-empt the Comet. The British Government leaned unashamedly on the Australian Government.

The Qantas evaluation of Comet 1 was that, with Ghost engines, it did not have a chance on the Kangaroo Route. Comet 2 would be marginal and probably fail. Qantas executive pilots who flew the various Comets and Britannias flagged handling as the main concern, while the airline's technical evaluation department raised doubts about de Havilland's engineering philosophy in the design of the Comet's structure. The British reaction was to condemn the Qantas team as biased against the Comet in particular and British aircraft in general. The implication in political circles was that Qantas was disloyal to the British Commonwealth. But losses of three Comets in subsequent accidents showed that the Australians were 'ruthlessly right', as one BOAC executive later admitted.

Eventually, BOAC withdrew its objections to the Qantas choice of the Super Constellation. Back home the Government approved an order for five Super Constellations (L1049Cs), shortly to be followed by three more, for delivery in 1954 and early 1955.

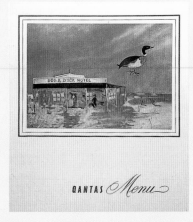

QANTAS *Menu*

ABOVE: 1950s Qantas Menu, showing the painting *The Dog and Duck* by Sidney Nolan.
BELOW: Capacity flown (millions of ton miles) graph, from the 1955 Qantas Empire Airways Ltd annual report.

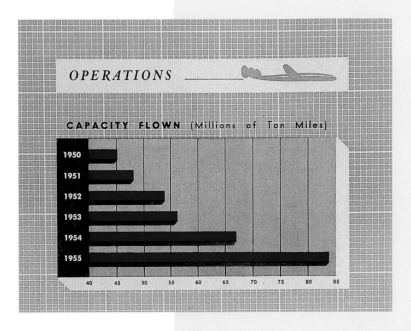

OPERATIONS

CAPACITY FLOWN (Millions of Ton Miles)

1950	
1951	
1952	
1953	
1954	
1955	

40 45 50 55 60 65 70 75 80 85

OPPOSITE: A collage of 1950s
Qantas menus.

The Super Constellations went first onto the newly acquired Southern Cross route to the United States, to compete against Pan American's Douglas DC-7Cs (Seven Seas), with the inaugural flight taking place on 15 May 1954.

The pace within Qantas increased as C O Turner became general manager, then chief executive, and made more and more of the running, to the expressed anguish of Sir Hudson Fysh, who was chairman.

Frequency on the Pacific Southern Cross Route increased to three flights per week, while the bigger, new aircraft were also introduced onto the Kangaroo Route, to Hong Kong and eventually to Johannesburg as the L749s phased out.

The 'Super Connie' gave Qantas a powerful marketing tool, which it reinforced with high standards of service and reliability, despite what turned out to be temperamental engines on the bigger aircraft. On the Kangaroo Route, Qantas offered both First and Tourist Class travel as soon as the L1049s were inaugurated on the service from Sydney to London in 1954. The seating was varied according to demand, with one fully First Class flight a week, the 'Connoisseur Service', departing Sydney on Saturdays to serve the government and business travellers.

In almost a decade, fares had risen only slightly. The cost of a First Class return Sydney–London via Singapore fare on the new aircraft was the equivalent of $1,345, while the return Economy fare was $1,075. Although still high, this was more affordable than ever before. In terms of buying power, seven or eight years before, the cost of a return flight from Australia to the United Kingdom was prohibitive for the average person. Although fares were coming down slowly, air travel was still beyond the reach of most Australians—this was the age of the passenger ships that

MENU

Christmas... 1957

Appetiser

Lobster and Prawn Cocktail

Roast Yuletide Turkey with Chestnut Stuffing
Roast Potatoes
Brussel Sprouts — Minted Garden Peas
Iced Asparagus Spears
with Thousand Island Dressing
Green Salad with French Dressing

Traditional Christmas Pudding and Brandy Sauce
Mince Pies
Basket of Fresh Fruit

Chocolate   Candy
Mint
Coffee

Sherry

JUS D'ANANAS FRAPPE
Chilled Pineapple Juice

CORNFLAKES A LA CREME
Cornflakes with Cream

COMPOTE

menu

QANTAS — COCOS ISLANDS

QANTAS

MENU

QANTAS

ABOVE: A section of the instrument panel on a Super Constellation.

came to Australia carrying migrants from Europe and returned with many young Australians looking for wider horizons.

Perth had been added to the route in 1955, when the frequency was three services a week. The following year, there were four services taking in the West, with a fifth added later in the year.

The bigger aircraft offered considerably more seats each week. BOAC, the revenue-sharing partner on the route, offered matching frequencies, although it was to use the L749 for a longer period than Qantas after disasters with the Comets forced the jet's withdrawal. BOAC also complemented the Qantas routes, offering ports such as Rangoon and Zurich, and opening up a wide choice to travellers within the overall BOAC–Qantas partnership.

A ROUND-THE-WORLD SERVICE

The Australian Government had held talks with the United States Government, seeking rights across America and the Atlantic to London, which would give Qantas a round-the-world route. The talks succeeded in 1957 when the Australian side pointed out that the Kangaroo Route went over a number of countries in Asia and the Middle East at that time prone to war and insurrection. The American side secured sweeping extra rights from Australia for Pan American in the exchange.

Qantas became a world commercial aviation leader in December 1957, only 10 years after its first Constellation flight to London, when the Super Constellation *Southern Aurora* departed on a 43,000-kilometre proving flight round the world carrying 32 media representatives. The party met Presidents and Prime Ministers, religious leaders (including the Pope and the Archbishop of Canterbury), ministers from various governments, and industry leaders. The following month—on 14 January 1958—two Super Constellations departed Melbourne: the *Southern Aurora* flew east, and the *Southern Zephyr* west. They both arrived in Sydney for a second ceremony, flew in formation over the city then banked off on their two courses, eventually meeting again in London.

The dual round-the-world services enabled Qantas to quote two fares to London: the normal one over Singapore; and a second over New York, which cost the equivalent of about $50 more than the shorter journey.

As Qantas prepared for the introduction of the first of its jets, the Boeing 707-138s at the end of the 1950s, it had established a reputation to be proud of. The outback airline had blossomed, in only three and a half decades, into the first round-the-world carrier. Despite the handicaps of unreliable engines and the need to carry big flight crews on the long journeys, Qantas had built up a name for service and friendliness that appealed to travellers of all kinds. Yet, as the airline signed contracts for the jets that were bigger and faster than any aircraft they had previously envisaged, only a handful of visionaries in the airline industry could predict the huge changes that lay ahead.

BELOW: 'Farewell to the Connies'. The last of 668 Wright Cyclone R3350–TC18DA series engines overhauled at the Qantas maintenance base at Mascot.

INTRODUCING THE JET ERA

The first Boeing 707 jets launched another era for Qantas and the Kangaroo Route.

The first Boeing 707 jets launched another era for Qantas and the Kangaroo Route. They carried 50 per cent more passengers at twice the speed.

When the 707s came into service in November 1959, they operated in parallel with Super Constellations. The piston-engine aircraft schedule was for a 1.45 pm departure from Sydney on Sundays and a 7.40 am (local time) landing in London on Tuesdays. The 707 flight departing at 1 pm on Saturdays arrived in London at 4.15 the next afternoon. The Super Constellations cruised at up to 20,000 feet (6,100 metres), which took them into the tops of the towering storm clouds in the monsoon regions. The new jets operated at 33,000 feet (about 10,000 metres) and higher, which was well above most of the weather.

The 707s, with their swept-back wings and high approach speeds, required new flying skills and also advanced engineering support. But they quickly achieved a degree of reliability that was significantly higher than any predecessor. One of the main reasons was the simplicity of the jet engine compared with the extreme complexity of the ultimate piston engines. In a speech to airline colleagues at a conference in Seattle in the mid-1960s (and with four years of 707 experience behind him), Captain Ritchie compared the reliability of the Curtis Wright compound engines in the L1049 with the Pratt and Whitney JTD-7s in the Boeings. In 1958, the last full year of Super Constellation operations, Qantas experienced 58 premature engine removals en route, compared with three for the jet fleet in 1963. The number of piston engines removed and completely overhauled at base was 71, compared with no jet engines. And there had been 136 engine

ABOVE: A 70th anniversary poster featuring a 747 over Sydney Harbour.
BELOW: Qantas jet bags are now collector's items.
OPPOSITE PAGE: A replica of the company's first aircraft, the Avro 504K alongside a 707 V-Jet at Sydney Airport.

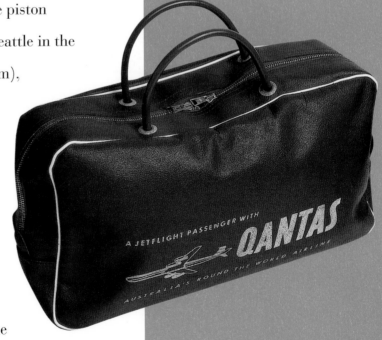

shutdowns during flight with the L1049, compared with only 13 for the Boeing 707. Not stated, but obvious to Captain Ritchie's professional audience, was the huge consequent saving in costs and the commercial advantage in reliably maintaining schedules without engineering delays.

Rather than reaching a plateau, the technology cycle seemed to speed up with the introduction of the Boeing 707-138 jets in June 1959. A higher performance version of the standard aircraft, it was about three metres shorter than the standard 707 and had more powerful engines, enabling Qantas to use the jet aircraft out of short, high-temperature runways, such as that in Nadi, Fiji.

The first engines were turbo jets—noisy, smoky and thirsty for fuel. A development by Pratt and Whitney made it possible to modify the engines so that a fan at the front drew in air and passed it around the main casing, encompassing the jet stream. This reduced fuel consumption, increased thrust and reduced noise. Qantas was able to undertake the modification in its Jet Base at Mascot, which was a remarkable achievement for a remote centre, comparable with the early Q.A.N.T.A.S. feat of building its own biplanes at

Longreach in the 1920s. Qantas was among the world's first airlines to fly the 707 with the advanced engine (it was designated the 707-138B and branded the 'V-Jet'—after *vannus*, Latin for 'fan'). The superior performance and range of the Boeing 707-138Bs provided further commercial advantage in terms of reliability and route flexibility.

Between 1959 and 1964, Qantas took delivery of 13 of the smaller jets. Soon, growing passenger and freight requirements, and the promise of greater range, led the airline to trade them in on 21 of the bigger 707-300s (designated the '-338C'). Qantas was to lease one more and acquire a 23rd second-hand. Between 1967 and 1969 the smaller Boeings were either traded in or sold, attracting a premium in the international airline market.

ABOVE: Boeing 707 V-Jet at Sydney Airport.
BELOW: 'How the V-Jet engine works' brochure which described the workings of the 'new generation' fan jet engines.

ROUTES WITH A DIFFERENCE

The longer range of the modified and new jets opened up adventurous new routes. The traditional gateway of Darwin was bypassed on the Kangaroo Route and Jakarta relegated to a minor halt. Fiji was also to be flown over except on tourist services. Among the route options that became possible on the Kangaroo were Hong Kong and the northern Middle East (added in 1964) and through Bangkok instead of Singapore. At the beginning of 1961 there were three jet and two Super Constellation flights a week. In 1964 there were six 707 flights a week (with BOAC operating parallel Comet 4s). And in 1967 (when Brisbane had been added to the Australian departure points), the number of 707 flights shot

IT'S ALL QUITE SIMPLE, REALLY!

HOW A REVOLUTIONARY V-JET ENGINE WORKS

DOUBLE NORMAL AIR INTAKE

EXTRA FLOW OF COOL AIR AROUND ENGINE FOR GREATER THRUST

V-Jet is the name conceived by Qantas for its aircraft engines powered by the fan-jet engines. The whole Qantas Boeing fleet is to be equipped with these engines. The "V" symbol is the Qantas abbreviation of the Latin word "Vannus" meaning fan, and it is the addition of these fans which gives the new engine its power, as explained in the illustration at left.

AUSTRALIA'S ROUND-THE-WORLD AIRLINE QANTAS

PRINTED IN AUSTRALIA

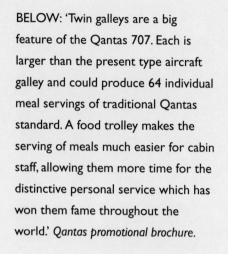

up to 11 a week, which increased to 23 in 1971, just before the much bigger 747 was introduced. A new round-the-world route was also developed in 1966 through Tahiti and Mexico to Bermuda and London with two flights a week.

The new routes were not the only element of adventure on Qantas flights of the 1960s. Practical jokes were often played by experienced crew to 'initiate' novices. Colin Burgess, a serving flight service director and author, tells how one novice flight attendant, giving his first safety demonstration, placed the life jacket over his head and found, at the appropriate moment, that the inflation tags were tied together. He pulled at the right tag—and it inflated. Someone had substituted the real thing for the demonstration model. Then came the oxygen mask. Synchronising with the recorded announcement, he placed it over his nose and mouth and breathed normally. Someone had filled

the mask with Vegemite. By this time passengers were rolling in the aisles with laughter. One last task remained before he could escape: to produce the safety card. When he unfolded it, a Playboy centrefold leapt into view!

This era was characterised by increasing prosperity and, as earnings rose and fares declined, the prospect of air travel fell within reach of more Australians. For many of them, the long sea voyage to Europe was steadily replaced by Qantas services on the Kangaroo route.

When the first jets were introduced internationally, many airlines charged a jet surcharge. In the early 1960s Qantas offered the same fares on both types of aircraft. The First Class return fare to London (via Singapore) had risen to the equivalent of $1,755 ($1,170 in Economy).

With the jets came new technologies. The need for radio operators was eliminated by improved communications. The spread of very high frequency (VHF) communications improved quality, while improvements in high frequency (HF) voice allowed Morse transmissions to be superseded, with the pilots taking over the communications work. This included making regular position reports by voice as they were flying over oceans and continents.

BELOW: 'Amongst the many improvements in facilities for passengers in the Qantas 707 is the provision of five de-luxe toilet rooms; two forward and three aft. New plastic materials, stainless steel fittings, and large illuminated mirrors are featured.' *Qantas promotional brochure.*

SPORTS RESULTS 1967–76

WIMBLEDON MEN'S SINGLES

Year	Winner	Runner-up	Score
1967	J D Newcombe (3)	W P Bungett	6-3, 6-1, 6-1
1968	R G Laver (1)	A D Roche (15)	6-3, 6-4, 6-2
1969	R G Laver (1)	J D Newcombe (6)	6-4, 5-7, 6-4, 6-4
1970	J D Newcombe (2)	K R Rosewall (5)	5-7, 6-3, 6-2, 3-6, 6-1
1971	J D Newcombe (2)	S R Smith (4)	6-3, 5-7, 2-6, 6-4, 6-4
1972	S R Smith (1)	I Nastase (2)	4-6, 6-3, 6-3, 4-6, 7-5
1973	J Kodes (2)	A Metreveli (4)	6-1, 9-8, 6-3
1974	J S Connors (3)	K R Rosewall (9)	6-1, 6-1, 6-4
1975	A R Ashe (6)	J S Connors (1)	6-1, 6-1, 5-7, 6-4
1976	B R Borg (4)	I Nastase (3)	6-4, 6-2, 9-7

ENGLISH DERBY

Year	Winner	Jockey
1967	Royal Palace	G Moore
1968	Sir Ivor	L Piggott
1969	Blakeney	E Johnson
1970	Nijinsky	L Piggott
1971	Mill Reef	G Lewis
1972	Roberto	L Piggott
1973	Morston	E Hide
1974	Snow Knight	B Taylor
1975	Grundy	P Eddery
1976	Empery	L Piggott

MELBOURNE CUP

Year	Winner	Jockey
1967	Red Handed	R Higgins
1968	Rain Lover	J Johnson
1969	Rain Lover	J Johnson
1970	Baghdad Note	E J Didham
1971	Silver Knight	R B Marsh
1972	Piping Lane	J Letts
1973	Gala Supreme	F Reys
1974	Think Big	H White
1975	Think Big	H White
1976	Van Der Hum	R J Skelton

RUGBY UNION SERIES RECORDS - ENGLAND V AUSTRALIA

Year	Venue	Winners	Score
1967	Twickenham	Australia	23-11
1973	Twickenham	England	20-3
1975	Sydney	Australia	16-9
	Brisbane	Australia	30-21
1976	Twickenham	England	23-6

TEST CRICKET RECORDS - ENGLAND V AUSTRALIA

Season	Tests	England	Australia	Draw	Ashes Held By
1968	5	1	1	3	Australia
1972	5	2	2	1	England
1974-75	6	1	4	1	Australia
1975	4	0	1	3	Australia

New technologies also brought the beginning of the end for the 'Vascos'. The first 707s had a periscope for the navigator to take his sun and star sights, but this was to become obsolete in later models. The first step in the mid-1960s was the introduction of Doppler radar, which tracked the aircraft's speed and direction over the ground and greatly improved the accuracy of dead reckoning. Eventually the civil airlines adopted inertial navigation systems (INS), which measured speed and course alterations with such a high degree of accuracy that, at the end of an eight-hour flight, the INS would be accurate to within about 15 nautical miles (less than 30 kilometres). In operation, Qantas installed three separate INS in each aircraft for reliability and accuracy. With this equipment, navigators were dropped from the crews. The proud Qantas skills of astro-navigation had become a thing of the past.

The problem that faced the airlines was when or whether they should order the new supersonic transports (SSTs), which promised to cut journey times in half and change the air transport industry as dramatically as the introduction of jets had done. The brief promise of supersonic transports failed to materialise, however, except for the highly subsidised British Airways and Air France Concorde. The American SST program, in which Qantas was also interested, was abandoned. The next move was into bigger aircraft, carrying more passengers and ushering in the era of mass travel.

As the 1970s approached, Qantas appeared to have reached a peak of success. Its Boeing 707s, sporting the kangaroo emblem on their tails, were a familiar sight at airport terminals in Asia, Europe and North America. The airline's main strength was still its Kangaroo Route between Australia and London. But Qantas was a true round-the-world airline on two distinct routes: one across the United States, the other across Mexico. Both, of course, crossed the Atlantic to London—the Kangaroo Route terminus and Australia's traditional link with Europe.

Inside Qantas a new guard was moving into positions of authority. Its members were conscious of the rapidly changing world of airline politics, competition and national outlook, in part arising from the huge migrations of the 1950s and '60s. Qantas celebrated its 50th birthday in March 1970, and the Queen and Duke of Edinburgh began a tour of Australia that included a visit to a Qantas exhibition at Longreach. Symbolising the dichotomy that was to develop in Qantas, in June, Sir Roland Wilson, recipient of an imperial title, was reappointed chairman for a further three years.

On the management side, Sir Cedric Turner and Captain Bert Ritchie, an aviation professional with technical training, had taken over. Under Ritchie, Qantas came of age—operationally, in management, in engineering and in marketing.

BELOW: The once ubiquitous Qantas bag has become something of an icon in its own right, keenly sought by collectors of Australian nostalgia.

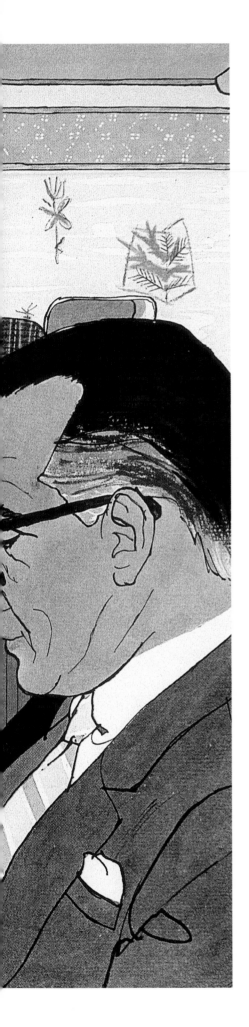

For Qantas the 1970s were a decade of continuous change and challenge. The Whitlam Government brought profound changes to the nation and thus to the market for Kangaroo Route travel. Globally, huge increases in fuel prices threatened Qantas and other international carriers.

UNIVERSAL TURMOIL

When Bert Ritchie took over, the world economy was turning down and an economic crisis was developing in the airline industry. Some airlines were digging their own financial graves and rivals, like Pan American, were in the process of disappearing. Despite falling passenger numbers, the airlines were adding new, big aircraft and consequently costly excess capacity.

Just as the Australian demand for travel began to grow, charter operators, not burdened with scheduled overheads, and using cheaper, older aircraft, began advertising lower fares, particularly out of Europe. Many Australians wanted to visit Asia and the Pacific region for short holidays. Others, including the first wave of postwar migrants to Australia, wanted to visit their homelands or to bring relatives to Australia. There was strong pressure on the Australian Government to allow these charter airlines to offer lower air fares to the public.

At Qantas, costs were soaring and wages eventually reached the point where they represented 35 per cent of the airline's expenditure. There was

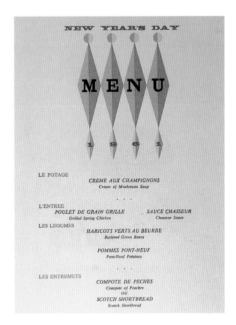

NEW YEAR'S DAY

MENU

1961

LE POTAGE
CREME AUX CHAMPIGNONS
Cream of Mushroom Soup

L'ENTREE
POULET DE GRAIN GRILLE   SAUCE CHASSEUR
Grilled Spring Chicken   Chasseur Sauce
LES LEGUMES
HARICOTS VERTS AU BEURRE
Buttered Green Beans

POMMES PONT-NEUF
Pont-Neuf Potatoes

LES ENTREMETS
COMPOTE DE PECHES
Compote of Peaches
OU
SCOTCH SHORTBREAD
Scotch Shortbread

ABOVE: Service with a smile 1970s style on board a 747.

heavy spending on infrastructure, including computers, to handle first message-switching, then reservations. War in the Middle East led to route diversions.

Qantas had been dipping a toe into the waters of charter with migrant carriage, on its own aircraft and on planes hired from British Caledonian. In 1971 these flights carried some 71,000 passengers (the total number on all services was 790,000), about half of whom were migrants. Qantas believed the only way to provide lower fares was on scheduled services. The early charter experience, blended with capacity on scheduled flights, provided the basis on which Qantas launched its own low-fare holiday program with resounding success the following year.

While the charter issue flared in media controversy and simmered in debates within government departments and within Qantas, fundamental changes were taking place in the airline. For the first time a senior executive, Keith Hamilton, then 40, was appointed to run day-to-day operations. He had a legendary reputation inside the airline industry but was little known outside.

Australia, meanwhile, was getting ready to enter the next era of commercial aviation with the advent of widebody aircraft.

In mid-1971, as the world's airline industry wallowed in depression, Qantas took delivery of its first Boeing 747—an aircraft which would revolutionise air travel for passengers and the airline, just as the Constellation and the Boeing 707 had done before.

The maiden flight of the Boeing 747 had taken place in the United States some 18 months before Qantas received its first of the widebody aircraft. The acquisition by Qantas was a traditionally considered judgement, the airline's management preferring to wait for an aircraft which more adequately met its unique long-range requirements.

Calling on its close relationship with Boeing following the purchase of the 707s, Qantas took a leading role with the manufacturer to develop further the basic design to improve the 747's payload-range capabilities and engine reliability. These changes were embodied in the 747, the first of which—VH-EBA *City of Canberra* —arrived in Sydney to a tumultuous welcome on 16 August 1971.

Qantas became the lead customer for the 747 aircraft, once more setting the pace for the world's long-range operators.

In September 1971 Qantas introduced the new aircraft on the Kangaroo Route, first to Singapore and then to London. That year an estimated 16,000 Australians had taken charter aircraft from Singapore rather than pay full fares. Qantas had to trim staff, standing down first air and cabin crew because of the reduced number of flights, and later ground crew as well.

Qantas tried to isolate two markets and capture them with targeted fares. The first initiative was the Pacesetter Fare, aimed at the youth market in 1970. It was a one-way fare available to London over either Singapore ($390) or New York or Mexico ($405). The second was an Affinity Group Fare, introduced in 1972, which was targeted at the market that was turning to charter operators. It was available only as a return to London, with a number of restrictions, at a cost of $730.20. It was the start of the era of low-fare and mass travel. Within three months

ABOVE: A model shows off a new Qantas uniform.
BELOW: A promotional brochure.

QANTAS PRESENTS
THE *Woman's Angle*
ON OVERSEAS AIR TRAVEL

AUSTRALIA'S
ROUND-THE-WORLD AIRLINE

BARRY HUMPHRIES

Barry Humphries is an outstanding Australian performer of his generation. He contrives to combine high intellect and low comedy to create a gallery of outrageously satirical characters who include the suburban supermum Dame Edna Everage, the bibulous cultural ambassador Sir Les Patterson and the chronic nostalgic Sandy Stone.

'Many pale London folk to whom a trip to the Isle of Wight seems overlong, shudder when I tell them I'm popping off to Australia.

'"But it only takes a day," I tell them, "and all you need is a good book." Not even that these days, since there are all those movies on tap, which in the normal run of things, you wouldn't cross the road to see.

'But doesn't every journey take a day? Even a trip into the West End from an outlying London suburb is an arduous day's work, so why not go to Melbourne instead? I was, of course, educated as a traveller on the famous Kangaroo Route. It took a bit longer in the old days, but it was always fun up there in those cosy aircraft with their reassuring vinyl appointments. I spent most of every flight, when the other passengers were asleep, with their slumber shades (grey terry towelling?) and their "don't wake me for cocktails" stickers, chatting and sharing jokes with those affable pink-jacketed Qantas stewards who all had the most keenly developed sense of humour in the world. When we stopped at Singapore, we'd all go shopping together, and over a cup of tea at Raffles they would introduce me to their colleagues who would be taking over on my next leg.

'Those marvellous "flight attendants" of yesteryear had seen it all, and since then have even published some amusing booklets of their less scandalous reminiscences. There was the couple they discovered one night in the most intimate of human connections in the middle of the first-class aisle, just as breakfast was about to be served. The male participant was not, of course, the Prime Minister, but a distinguished politician at very few removes from our then Leader. And they keep telling me Les Patterson is over the top!'

the steady decline of traffic had been reversed. Even so, Qantas had to report a loss of $6 million for the 1971–72 financial year. After the new, low fares, the September 1972 schedules saw a planned increase in 747 flights on the Kangaroo Route from three to five a week and a reduction in stops, reducing the flight time to less than 25 hours.

MORE THAN A MILLION PASSENGERS

Heartened by the success of the low-fare initiatives to Europe, Qantas and Malaysia–Singapore Airlines (MSA) launched a daring holiday program to Asia in 1972. Inclusive tours on special 707 flights (designated 'charters') offered a week in Singapore for under $300, with an additional week in Malaysia available for an extra $100. The original program was designed to fill 6,000 seats. It proved so successful that another 4,000 were placed on the market and snapped up. The annual report for the year ended 31 March 1973 listed a modest profit of $466,000, a dramatic turnaround. In calendar year 1973, Qantas was to carry more than one million passengers for the first time, a 28 per cent increase on the previous year. In the next financial year, profit rose to $11.1 million.

The success of the Asian holiday program led to wider inclusive tour holiday marketing. Low fares to Britain and Europe produced almost 50 per cent traffic growth on the route in the first year, and 25 per cent in the second. The planning was for continued growth of 20 per cent by 1975–76. Qantas decided to move entirely to 747s on the Kangaroo Route, to take advantage of its lower costs, estimated at the time to be about 13 per cent below those of the 707.

When Wilson, the part-time chairman, became ill in July 1973, the Government appointed Sir Donald Anderson, the Director General of Civil Aviation, to succeed him on a full-time basis. Sir Hudson Fysh, co-founder of the airline, and chairman until 1966, died in April 1974.

In the mid-1970s, the oil-producing countries not only lifted their prices, but raised them repeatedly. Airlines faced an immense

ABOVE: A Qantas menu, showing information about Australian wines.
BELOW: Qantas menu–'Australia's round-the-world airline'.

The Boeing 707s introduced a new era of faster travel, comfort and convenience. Here, First Class passengers on one of the early 707-138s enjoy a silver service entrée.

jump in operating costs. This coincided in Australia with a burst of wage inflation, presenting Qantas with a financial crisis. The expansionary budget for 1974–75 had predicted a profit of $9.7 million. Within weeks, this plummeted to an estimated loss of $10 million.

INFLATION STRIKES

In 1975 the full effects of fuel prices and resulting worldwide inflation hit international airlines. Qantas estimated that its wage bill had risen by $40 million and its fuel bill by $30 million. The only way to compensate for this was to increase both fares and the seating on 747s to 10 abreast in Economy Class. To fill the extra capacity, Qantas surged into low-cost travel. After agreements with six Asian airlines, Qantas offered excursion fares to major Asian cities at discounts of 30 to 40 per cent off normal economy fares.

Mass, low-cost air travel had arrived in Australia at a time of inflationary pressure and political instability. On the Kangaroo Route to the United Kingdom–Europe, Qantas had carried 40,000 passengers in 1971–72. In the year ended 31 March 1975, the total was 255,000.

Yet it was a profitless boom. In the following year, to 31 March 1976, Qantas would report a loss of $14.1 million, moderated by a profit on the sale of three Boeing 707 aircraft, which brought in $7 million. Sir Donald, stricken by ill health, resigned and died soon afterwards. He was succeeded by Sir Lenox Hewitt as full-time chairman, in August 1975.

MASS-MARKET COMPETITION

The year 1976 was a time of crisis for Qantas. Management under Ritchie had begun the process of reinventing the airline: it had moved from providing a service to the elite, prepared to pay high prices, to being a competitor in the mass market, bidding for the discretionary consumer dollar.

In March 1976 Ritchie reached retirement age and the board appointed Keith Hamilton as general manager. Ritchie handed over to a new, postwar generation with an international outlook. Along with the knighthoods bestowed on Ritchie's predecessors, many aspects of the airline's international links became nostalgic relics. Far from providing a service for the elite, Qantas now chased the lowest seat–mile costs that only big aircraft could provide, and looked for efficiencies in every aspect of the business.

The expansionary dreams of the 1960s could not survive in an era of mass travel and high costs. Ritchie bequeathed to Hamilton an airline that was completely different in outlook from the one he had inherited from Turner. Hamilton and his successors had the task of transforming it once again.

As fuel costs settled down and the Australian economy revived, the chairman, Sir Lenox Hewitt, was able to report the 1976–77 profit of $11.8 million (a dramatic turnaround from the previous year's loss of $14.2 million) and pointed the finger at the burden of high wages in Australia. An average employee, he wrote, cost Qantas (in 1977) $15,569 per annum, British Airways $8,782, Singapore Airlines $6,841 and Air New Zealand $8,620.

ABOVE: 'Right around the world by Qantas' illustration used in a promotional brochure.

The competition from foreign carriers, particularly Asian airlines such as Singapore Airlines lying across the Kangaroo Route, made inroads into Australian-originating traffic, which under the traditional rules had been a Qantas 'entitlement'.

Hamilton persuaded the Government to enforce the traditional rules, regulating fares and agent commissions and trying to block the Asians from access to Australia–United Kingdom/Europe through traffic. The Department of Transport evolved an International Civil Aviation Policy (ICAP). The policy ordered Asian carriers such as Singapore Airlines to restrict the number of services to its traffic entitlements. Singapore and its ASEAN allies strenuously objected and a war of words raged between the Australian and Singapore Governments as well as between the two national airlines.

The airline was still profitable but cost increases at the end of the 1970s led to an overall loss of $21.2 million in 1979–80. On the equipment level, directors and management worked towards giving Qantas the most efficient fleet possible—an all-747 fleet that was to convert to the more economic Rolls-Royce engine. By 1979 the last of the Boeing 707-338Cs would be retired. They were to succeed in 1977–78 in reporting the highest profit up to that time, of just under $16 million.

ABOVE: A 40th anniversary menu.
BELOW: The Qantas 707-138 *City of Sydney*.

LEANER, TOUGHER, SMARTER

CHAPTER EIGHT

Over the years, the Kangaroo Route had spread throughout Asia and Europe.

Over the years, the Kangaroo Route had spread throughout Asia and Europe. Once a thin stream between Sydney and London, through Singapore, India, Pakistan, the Middle East and southern Europe, Kangaroo Route runnels had broadened north through Manila and Hong Kong, through New Delhi in northern India, to Tehran and into central Europe through ports such as Vienna and Frankfurt. Another stream went to Bangkok and Middle East ports such as Bahrain, then to Athens and Rome. As the traffic developed in the 1980s, one channel through Amsterdam went to Manchester.

Back home, Sydney no longer remained the sole source of traffic. Flights began from Melbourne as Tullamarine Airport celebrated its 10th birthday. Perth and Brisbane also became feeders, first as way points of flights from Sydney and Melbourne, then as starting points in their own right. In the early 1980s Adelaide also came on stream.

The schedules of the day mapped the Kangaroo Route like the braided streams of the Channel Country of western Queensland, starting singly then spreading out over the floodplain before consolidating into a final broad river which poured into London. From the 1960s to the mid-1980s, Qantas inaugurated port after port in Europe, partly because of the demand from former migrants, who were now settled in Australia and wanted to return home for visits. It was this market that charter operators tried to tap; and Qantas scheduled the flights to hold these competitors at bay.

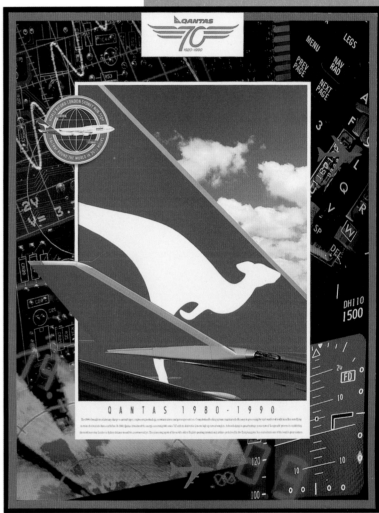

ABOVE: A poster commemorating the airline's 70th anniversary.
OPPOSITE PAGE: Cargo by the container load goes into the 747's hold.

ROUTE CONSOLIDATION

At the end of the 1980s, however, that diffuse pattern of routes consolidated. Qantas took advantage of the growing market volumes and technical improvements in its Boeing 747s—plus the introduction of Boeing 767s—to return the Kangaroo Route to its banks. Qantas drastically cut back the number of destinations in Europe. It abandoned or reduced services through Athens, Istanbul, Vienna, Belgrade, Rome, Paris, Amsterdam and Manchester; and it began increasingly to service Asian ports with direct flights from Australia, while moving to establish a 'golden triangle' route network in Asia itself. The Kangaroo Route 'river' was shorter and more direct; but with the huge increase in traffic it was deeper, broader and flowed faster than ever.

And there were other factors in the consolidation. The 1980s inherited the economic depression and uncertainty of the 1970s. Rising wage costs in Australia, along with higher costs of both fuel and financing new aircraft, continued, coinciding with greater competition from the young airlines of South-East Asia. The traditional system of regulated fares and controlled capacity withered away.

LEFT: Modern Singapore—the high-grade facilities of its Changi Airport allowed Qantas to use it as a hub airport to more passengers arriving on flights from different Australian cities to diverse Asian and European destinations.

There was also physical change in the aircraft themselves. The Qantas flagship was the Boeing 747, which during the 1980s was reconfigured to provide 400 seats on every flight. This was too much capacity to puddle-jump in the traditional pattern of the Kangaroo Route. As the 747 developed, it also acquired immense range so that it could fly from Sydney to London in two hops.

To deal with all this, Qantas developed a new strategy. The market wanted direct flights out of the smaller capitals such as Adelaide and Perth. As the Boeing 767 fleet grew, Qantas used the twin-jet to serve these capitals, which could profitably carry smaller loads that were not profitable on the 747s.

ABOVE: Jim Leslie was appointed a director in October 1979, chairman in July 1980, and resigned from the Board in November 1989. BELOW: Keith Hamilton joined Qantas in 1948, becoming general manager in 1976 and a director and chief executive in 1980. OPPOSITE PAGE: The 747–400.

CRUCIAL INNOVATIONS

As well, Qantas became a lively innovator. It launched Business Class internationally, which proved an immediate success—and which virtually every other airline copied. And it was probably the first airline to develop the concept of an offshore hub. In the United States, about the same time, airlines had started 'hubbing'—flying into a central location and dispersing traffic to feeder flights out to smaller destinations. Qantas chose Singapore as its first hub (later it was to use Bangkok as well, on the Kangaroo Route, and Honolulu on the Pacific). The high-grade facilities of Singapore's Changi Airport allowed Qantas to fly in 747s from Sydney and Melbourne headed for destinations such as London and Frankfurt. At the same hectic time every evening would come 767s that had started, say, in Adelaide and flown via Darwin, direct from Perth or from Brisbane via Townsville or Cairns. After a short stopover at Singapore, the 747s from Australia flew on to Europe while the 767s sat on the ground waiting for incoming 747s from Europe and traffic from other parts of Asia. Then the dance would begin again—to sort out passengers, baggage and cargo for Australian destinations. The inbound 747s would fly to Sydney and Melbourne and the 767s to the smaller capitals.

But these were not the best of times for innovation. A deepening recession in Australia froze domestic economic activity, while in the airline industry worldwide aircraft were flying with thousands of empty seats and financially the industry was bleeding. Qantas carriage on the Kangaroo Route was down 10 per cent in the first four months of the 1980–81 financial year.

The economic position of Qantas deteriorated through 1981. The financial results for that year were a blow, a loss of $19.5 million, which

SPORTS RESULTS 1977–86

WIMBLEDON MEN'S SINGLES

Year	Winner	Runner-up	Score
1977	B R Borg (2)	J S Connors (1)	3-6, 6-2, 6-1, 5-7, 6-4
1978	B R Borg (1)	J S Connors (2)	6-2, 6-2, 6-3
1979	B R Borg (1)	L R Tanner (5)	6-7, 6-1, 3-6, 6-3, 6-4
1980	B R Borg (1)	J P McEnroe (2)	1-6, 7-3, 6-3, 6-7, 8-6
1981	J P McEnroe (2)	B R Borg (1)	4-6, 7-6, 7-6, 6-4
1982	J S Connors (2)	J P McEnroe (1)	3-6, 6-3, 6-7, 7-6, 6-4
1983	J P McEnroe (2)	C J Lewis (U)	6-2, 6-2, 6-2
1984	J P McEnroe (1)	J S Connors (3)	6-1, 6-1, 6-2
1985	B F Becker (U)	K M Curren (8)	6-3, 6-7, 7-6, 6-4
1986	B F Becker (4)	I Lendl (1)	6-4, 6-3, 7-5

ENGLISH DERBY

Year	Winner	Jockey
1977	The Minstrel	L Piggott
1978	Shirley Heights	G Starkey
1979	Troy	W Carson
1980	Henbit	W Carson
1981	Shergar	W Swinburn
1982	Golden Fleece	P Eddery
1983	Teenoso	L Piggott
1984	Secreto	C Roche
1985	Slip Anchor	S Cauthen
1986	Shahrastani	W Swinburn

MELBOURNE CUP

Year	Winner	Jockey
1977	Gold and Black	J Duggan
1978	Arwon	H White
1979	Hyperno	H White
1980	Beldale Ball	J Letts
1981	Just a Dash	P Cook
1982	Gurner's Lane	L Dittman
1983	Kiwi	J Cassidy
1984	Black Knight	P Cook
1985	What a Nuisance	P Hyland
1986	At Talaq	M Clarke

RUGBY UNION SERIES RECORDS - ENGLAND V AUSTRALIA

Year	Venue	Winners	Score
1976	Twickenham	England	23-6
1982	Twickenham	England	15-11
1984	Twickenham	Australia	19-3

TEST CRICKET RECORDS - ENGLAND V AUSTRALIA

Season	Tests	England	Australia	Draw	Ashes Held By
1977	5	3	0	2	England
1978-79	6	5	1	0	England
1981	6	3	1	2	England
1982-83	5	1	2	2	Australia
1985	6	3	1	2	England

included a loss on airline operations of $41 million.

Chief executive Keith Hamilton and newly appointed chairman Jim Leslie adopted an aggressive, commercial approach, particularly on the bitterly contested Kangaroo Route. The new Qantas policy was 'to fly our way out' of the recession with a new strategy to target competitors. In 1982 Qantas moved into the market with wholesale discounting, dropping some fares by up to $200 to experience encouraging growth again.

The Fraser Coalition Government was defeated in March 1983 and Kim Beazley became Minister for Aviation in the Labor Government. Qantas and the new minister established an early rapport, which was to enable the airline to conduct its business in a more commerical manner.

Irrespective, Qantas incurred a loss in 1982–83 of $34.4 million, with the loss on airline operations even higher, at $47.6 million. Fuel costs had risen by $44 million. The rise in traffic, thanks to aggressive marketing and the lower costs achieved by smaller staff numbers and control of operations, resulted in a profit for 1983–84 of just under $56 million from airline operations ($58.5 million for the group). Qantas, Leslie reported, was 'now a leaner, tougher and smarter airline'.

In 1984, Keith Hamilton died, and Ron Yates, the first Qantas engineer with an aeronautical engineering degree, was appointed chief executive.

THE THREE-MILLION MARK

By 1987 Boeing had committed to a new, long-range 747, the 400 model, with improved and more sophisticated avionics which would allow two-pilot operation. Boeing also planned to stretch the 767 to produce the 767-300ER, with equally long range. Riding on the crest of the traffic revival and new equipment during 1986, Qantas reported a record profit of $104.2 million in the year to 31 March 1987, carrying more than three million passengers in that period.

In mid-1987, the Australian travel market grew by almost 40 per cent and management had to charter flights from outside companies to carry the passengers.

The expansion of the Qantas Jet Base and the need to pay for the new aircraft required Qantas to seek $600 million in capital to maintain its balance sheet. Labor's then Transport Minister, Gareth Evans, took the daring step in 1988 of preparing a paper for the Labor caucus canvassing privatisation for the airline.

The board budgeted for a profit of $185 million in the 1988–89 financial year and $230 million in the following year. However, disaster came when Australia's domestic airlines were stopped by pilots, who resigned in August 1989 in a dispute over pay and conditions. The

BELOW: John Ward joined Qantas in 1969, becoming chief executive in 1989.

JILL HICKSON

Jill Hickson is a literary agent, representing some of the country's best and brightest authors. She was previously well-known in her role as International Relations Manager for Qantas. Jill is married to Neville Wran, who served a record 10 years as Premier of New South Wales.

'Flying throughout the world with Qantas gives you a true sense of your good fortune in being Australian; in having so many wonderful opportunities, not least the opportunity to travel. The very sight of the flying kangaroo on the tail of an aircraft brings a great surge of national pride, a sense of belonging, of family and home.

'The Kangaroo Route for me is synonymous with reading, the nourishment of mind and soul. The sheer luxury of those long stretches of time suspended in the realm of contemplation means that one's recall of books read on aeroplanes is extraordinarily vivid and long-lived.'

OPPOSITE PAGE: With a new emphasis on Asian routes, the Qantas 747 service reflected passengers' preferences.

country's thriving tourism industry suffered great disruption and Qantas revenues plunged with the uncertainty. It was in these circumstances that Leslie's term as chairman came to an end. His replacement was W L (Bill) Dix, former president and chief executive of the Ford Motor Company in Australia. In December, John Ward was named chief executive; it was the eve of celebrations of the airline's 70th anniversary.

Ward's first priority was to take urgent action to control Qantas costs as traffic and revenue fell in the aftermath of the domestic airline stoppage.

By the end of the decade, the Kangaroo Route had been streamlined in ways that would never have been thought possible in the pioneering Constellation days. As the new 747-400s phased in from late 1990, Qantas flew over the previous stops along the way, reducing the journey time to London to about 22 hours.

LEANER, TOUGHER, SMARTER

CHAPTER NINE

TOGETHER AGAIN

With the delivery of new-generation Boeing 747-438 Longreach aircraft imminent, Qantas was gaining the operational strength to consolidate...

With the delivery of new-generation Boeing 747-438 Longreach aircraft imminent, Qantas was gaining the operational strength to consolidate its position as one of the world's leading long-distance airlines.

Symbolic of the important role the new aircraft would play on the Kangaroo Route, Qantas flew its first 747-438—VH-OJA *City of Canberra*—18,000 kilometres non-stop from London to Sydney on its delivery flight from the manufacturer. Arriving in Sydney on 17 August 1989 after a record-breaking flight of 20 hours, nine minutes, -OJA was greeted by a crowd of media as well as the public. By this time it was widely recognised that the new machines would bring Australia and the United Kingdom even closer together.

When the 747-400s were introduced on the Kangaroo Route, the 23-hour, one-stop service to London was a graphic demonstration of the advances in aircraft technology that had been made on the route since 1947, when a full day's flying from Sydney transported passengers as far as Singapore—ahead of them, another three days and two nights to London.

It was somewhat ironic that, at a time when Qantas was taking delivery of the aircraft which would secure its future on long-haul operations, the global airline industry was floundering. The boom of the late 1980s spawned aircraft orders from the world's airlines which were being fulfilled just as profits began to tumble and worldwide demand dwindled. In addition, the Gulf War triggered oil price increases and airline revenues were further

ABOVE: A Qantas flight attendant helping a mother with her children.
BELOW: The chairman of Qantas, Gary Pemberton, with the chairman of British Airways, Sir Colin Marshall, in London in 1997.
LEFT: Children's *Max Pack* Qantas bag.
OPPOSITE PAGE: Qantas and British Airways staff in front of the Sydney Opera House.

• Following a world trend, Australia's stock market plunged 25 per cent on 20 October 1987, wiping $55 billion off traded shares.

• Australia celebrated its Bicentennial on 26 January 1988. The largest crowd assembled in the country—two million people—gathered around Sydney Harbour for the First Fleet commemorations.

• Australian naval forces joined the United Nations operation against Iraq after its invasions of Kuwait, the deployment on 14 August 1990 being the first of its kind in 20 years.

• The United Kingdom returned its Crown colony Hong Kong to mainland China on 30 June 1997.

• Diana, Princess of Wales, was killed in a car crash on Sunday 31 August 1997.

SPORT

• Australia retained the Ashes on 10 August 1997, winning them for a record fifth consecutive time.

• Australian athlete Cathy Freeman became the first Australian Aboriginal to win a World Championship medal when she won the 400 metres in Athens on 5 August 1997.

• Australian tennis player Patrick Rafter won the US Open on 7 September 1997.

POP CULTURE

• *Bran Nue Dae*, the exuberent musical by Aboriginal writer Jimmy Chi, had its world premiere at the 1990 Perth Festival.

• The internationally acclaimed artist Brett Whiteley, 53, died at Thirroul, New South Wales, on 15 June 1992.

• The star of *Shine*, Geoffrey Rush, won an Oscar for Best Actor at the 1997 Academy Awards in Hollywood.

---

further eroded. Between 1990 and 1993, the industry lost an estimated US$15.6 billion.

Individual airlines were galvanised into taking action against unprofitable operations and forced to improve efficiencies. Some of them did not make the transition and failed. Many of them were beginning to form strategic alliances with competitor airlines in the interests of long-term survival.

The worldwide recession of the early 1990s was no less severe in Australia. Although the ruinous strike by domestic airline pilots had not directly affected the airline's international operations, it had devastated inbound tourism and greatly curtailed business traffic on international services. Travellers could not get seats. Australia's leading business people and politicians had to be content with a webbing seat in the back of a Hercules military transport plane with coffee from a flask.

PRIVATISATION PLANS

The Australian Government proposed a number of measures to breathe new life into the nation's key industries, chief among which was its review of Australia's aviation industry. The 'One Nation' statement of February 1992 paved the way for

Qantas to return to the domestic market from which it had been excluded under the restrictive Two Airline Policy of 1946. The Government's new policy would also introduce competition on international routes from another Australian airline. More significantly, however, the Government decided that it would privatise Qantas.

In June 1992, the Government approved a $400-million bid by Qantas to acquire domestic operator Australian Airlines and its regional subsidiary airlines, readmitting it to the domestic market from whence it had originated more than 70 years before.

The Qantas purchase of Australian Airlines gave it the ability to offer travellers an unprecedented range of connecting domestic and international flights. Overnight Qantas added nearly 50 destinations to its network, and, though there was much work ahead of the airline to merge

BELOW: Qantas Boeing 747, *Wunala Dreaming*, one of two aircraft painted in Aboriginal colours and designs.

JOAN CARDEN

Joan Carden is one of only a few opera and concert singers who have achieved international renown while based in Australia. Travelling from this base, she has been acclaimed in Britain, the United States and continental Europe. She is a leader member of Opera Australia who holds both an AO and an OBE for her services to music.

'To fly the Kangaroo Route with Qantas is to enjoy one of the world's greatest journeys. I have been flying Qantas for more than 30 years. That's a lot of air miles and arias!

'But Qantas has always looked after me (and my voice). Qantas seems to understand that to sing opera, you need to be fit, well and rested. Generally it offers matchless service and safety-plus. On the occasions when I have been lucky enough to fly Qantas first class, I'm bound to say this becomes service and safety plus heaven!'

LEADING AIRPORT DESIGN

Qantas travellers are assured high levels of comfort and service on the ground and in the air. The airline's Sydney airport facilities at both the domestic and international terminals are being upgraded to the most advanced in Australia. As well as being visually attractive, the domestic terminal includes new valet parking facilities, enhanced levels of luxury and comfort from expanded Qantas Club lounges, plus new baggage handling and aerobridge technology. Companies including Airport Equipment, Glidepath and HH Robertson, have played a leading role in providing Qantas passengers with the last word in travel convenience and comfort at Australia's busiest airport.

the philosophically and operationally disparate operations, the Government now had a more attractive company to sell to private investors.

Meanwhile British Airways—which had been privatised in 1987—was seeking to expand its global reach. The new-found interest in co-operation between previously rival airlines was beginning to reshape the global aviation market.

While the Qantas brand was strong in its immediate region and on its long-established services to Asia, the United Kingdom and the Pacific—in particular, the west coast of the United States—the airline needed to find its niche in the emerging global market offered by airline alliances.

In 1992 the Australian Government issued an invitation for a 'trade' investor to buy a 25 per cent interest in Qantas as the first step to privatisation. Crucial in the process were the synergies that privatisation offered Qantas, in the light of its need to strengthen international

OPPOSITE PAGE: Qantas and British Airways held the first joint meeting of their Boards in London in July 1997. *Front row from left:* Robert Ayling, chief executive and director of BA and director of Qantas; Gary Pemberton, chairman, Qantas; Sir Colin Marshall, chairman, BA; James Strong, chief executive and director of Qantas; Sir Michael Angus, vice chairman, BA. Back row from left: Michael Davies, BA; the Hon. Raymond Seitz, BA; Trevor Kennedy, Qantas; Captain Colin Barnes, BA; Derek Stevens, chief financial officer, BA; Sir Robin Renwick, BA; Nick Tait,* Qantas; Mike Codd, Qantas; John Ducker, Qantas; Gary Toomey, chief financial officer, Qantas; Margaret Jackson, Qantas; Roger Maynard,* Qantas; Trevor Eastwood, Qantas; Dr Ashok S Ganguly, BA; Baroness O'Cathain, BA. Not present: Jim Kennedy, Qantas.

* Also executives of British Airways.

ADVANCED TECHNOLOGY

The intense competition in the aviation and travel industry during the 1990s has been matched by the commitment of Qantas to the most advanced technology from tailored application systems to the powerful computing hardware to run them.

The growth in passenger and freight movements and the continuing pressure on margins has seen Qantas remain focused on employing systems that guarantee operational safety and help deliver world-class customer service. To meet its operational and customer service requirements, Qantas works with a number of the world's leading information companies, in particular Unisys, which provides operational control, passenger services and customer loyalty functions.

The airline's latest investments in these areas, working with Unisys, are intended to ensure that safety and service continue to be the hallmarks of Qantas as we approach the next millennium.

ABOVE: Australian Air Express Pty Ltd (AaE) is a joint venture between Qantas Airways Limited and Australia Post Corporation. AaE was formed in 1992 and is today one of the nation's largest express freight service providers, maintaining and controlling an air freighter linehaul network of five jet aircraft and utilising the exclusive access of more than 250 Qantas passenger flights daily.

operations. In December 1992 the Australian Government announced that British Airways had won the bid for the 25 per cent shareholding. The deal allowed the two airlines to co-operate in relation to pricing, scheduling and marketing on the Kangaroo Route. The Qantas Board appointed accountants KPMG to give independent advice on the proposed financial arrangements.

The British carrier completed its $665 million investment in Qantas in March 1993, reuniting the former partners after 46 years. The subsequent formation of the alliance brought with it a 10-year commercial agreement which would fortify the airline's position in the global market.

The Qantas and British Airways world networks were largely complementary, meeting at common gateways in North America, Asia, Europe and southern Africa. British Airways brought to Qantas its strong

European and North Atlantic networks, and in turn the British airline's global network was strengthened by the comprehensive Qantas network of routes within the Asia–Pacific region. The successful flotation of Qantas, marked by its listing on the Australian Stock Exchange on 31 July 1995, raised $1.45 billion for the Australian Government. Qantas and British Airways were now ready to create a new future for their joint operations on the Kangaroo Route.

A NEW ALLIANCE

Although the two airlines had valuable experience in working together until the disbanding of the joint operation in 1947, their new relationship would, of necessity, be profoundly different. Now that they were no longer operating as instruments of their respective governments, their commercial imperatives were arguably stronger than at any other time in the history of their joint operations.

For airlines at this time, increasing competition was steadily eroding yields, creating a need to maximise efficiencies and cut costs. When Qantas began services to London in 1947, the average time taken to earn

BELOW: *Nalanji Dreaming*, the second Qantas 747 with an Aboriginal motif, departs Sydney Airport.

SPORTS RESULTS 1987-97

WIMBLEDON MEN'S SINGLES

Year	Winner	Runner-up	Score
1987	P H Cash (11)	I Lendl (2)	7-6, 6-2, 7-5
1988	S B Edberg (3)	B F Becker (6)	4-6, 7-6, 6-4, 6-2
1989	B F Becker (3)	S B Edberg (2)	6-0, 7-6, 6-4
1990	S B Edberg (3)	B F Becker (2)	6-2, 6-2, 3-6, 3-6, 6-4
1991	M D Stich (6)	B F Becker (2)	6-4, 7-6, 6-4
1992	A K Agassi (12)	G Ivanisevic (6)	6-7, 6-4, 6-4, 1-6, 6-4
1993	P Sampras (1)	J S Courier (3)	7-6, 7-6, 3-6, 6-3
1994	P Sampras (1)	G Ivanisevic (4)	7-6, 7-6, 6-0
1995	P Sampras (2)	B F Becker (3)	6-7, 6-2, 6-4, 6-2
1996	R P Krajicek (U)	M O Washington (U)	6-3, 6-4, 6-3
1997	P Sampras (1)	C Pioline (U)	6-4, 6-2, 6-4

ENGLISH DERBY

Year	Winner	Jockey
1987	Reference Point	S Cauthen
1988	Kahyasi	R Cochrane
1989	Nashwan	W Carson
1990	Quest For Fame	P Eddery
1991	Generous	A Munro
1992	Mr Devious	J Reid
1993	Commander In Chief	M Kinane
1994	Erhaab	W Carson
1995	Lammtarra	W Swinburn
1996	Shaamit	M Hills
1997	Benny The Dip	W Ryan

MELBOURNE CUP

Year	Winner	Jockey
1987	Kensei	L Olsen
1988	Empire Rose	T Allan
1989	Tawrrific	R S Dye
1990	Kingston Rule	D Beadman
1991	Let's Elope	S R King
1992	Subzero	G Hall
1993	Vintage Crop	M Kinane
1994	Jeune	W Harris
1995	Doriemus	D Oliver
1996	Saintly	D Beadman

RUGBY UNION SERIES RECORDS - ENGLAND V AUSTRALIA

Year	Venue	Winners	Score
1988	Brisbane	Australia	22-16
	Sydney	Australia	28-8
	Twickenham	England	28-19
1991	Sydney	Australia	40-15

TEST CRICKET RECORDS - ENGLAND V AUSTRALIA

Season	Tests	England	Australia	Draw	Ashes Held By
1986-87	5	2	1	2	England
1989	6	0	4	2	Australia
1990-91	5	0	3	2	Australia
1993	6	1	4	1	Australia
1994-95	5	1	3	1	Australia
1997	6	2	3	1	Australia

the lowest return fares was just under 130 weeks. By 1965 this had shrunk to 21 weeks, in 1985 to five weeks, and today to little more than three. In the face of rising costs and increasing competition from other airlines, the ability to compete and maintain economically viable operations on the Kangaroo Route was paramount for both Qantas and British Airways in the early 1990s.

A proposal developed by the airlines to meet these challenges was embodied in the Joint Services Agreement (JSA). The plan also offered travellers greater flexibility and an improved range of competitive fares, together with other benefits brought by better harnessing the combined resources of the companies.

In May 1995 the Australian Government approved the JSA for an initial five-year period, paving the way for co-ordinated scheduling, revenue and marketing on the 35 services operated each week by British Airways and Qantas on the Kangaroo Route. As a result, customers would enjoy greater benefits from the alliance through more competitive fares and a wider choice of travel options, opening up the possibility of travelling to Britain via Africa, north Asia or the United States.

Rationalisation and integration soon realised

savings for both airlines in the aircraft required to operate the Kangaroo services—for British Airways, the equivalent of one 747 and for Qantas approximately one 767. These aircraft were now available to operate on other parts of the airlines' networks and the immediate proof of co-operation through the JSA gave rise to impetus for more adventurous developments under the alliance.

Close co-operation on operational issues such as maintenance and engineering, ground support and airport operations were also important aspects of the alliance. The common gateways where Qantas and British Airways met became the first areas to benefit from the integration of resources. Joint airport operations now provide ground handling, line maintenance and customer services in Bangkok, Singapore, Taipei, Kuala Lumpur, Osaka and Nagoya. Joint sales offices have now been established in 16 cities around the world.

Qantas and British Airways have also developed joint lounges for Business and First Class passengers in key cities where the two airlines meet—namely, Bangkok, Singapore, Manila, Los Angeles and Hong Kong.

In another significant step forward, in October 1997 Qantas relocated its operations at London's Heathrow Airport from Terminal 3 to British Airways' intercontinental hub at Terminal 4. Qantas and British Airways passengers could now benefit from improved facilities when transferring between intercontinental and regional flights, and the move also gave the airlines an improved ability to streamline their operations at the European end of the route.

ABOVE: Hong Kong is one of several key destinations where Qantas and British Airways have developed joint lounges for their First and Business Class passengers.

THE QANTAS WARDROBE

The Qantas wardrobe is the familiar 'face' of Qantas that is seen by travellers and Qantas customers around the world. Its role in establishing and enhancing the image of Qantas has been so important the airline has always ensured the wardrobe's components provide durability and comfort for staff, as well as transmitting the quality and elegance that represents the Qantas name.

Various methods over the years have been employed to deliver the required wardrobe—from Parisian fashion designers to international manufacturers—so a truly world-class product was provided.

Today, the Australian fashion industry delivers one of the airline's most distinctive wardrobes, resulting from the close consultation between the airline, the designers and individual wardrobe component providers.

Of the thirteen key companies, each works in partnership with Qantas to deliver the specialist items that are regarded as the best in their class. But the differentiating strength evolves from the special relationships that each supplier also has developed with each of the other suppliers. They collectively deliver a total and integrated product, meeting Qantas' most exacting standards. The companies involved include Calcoup Knitwear, Corporate SF Clothing, George Gross and Harry Who, Ingewe, John Kaldor, Kolotex Australia, Luigi & Anthony, Macquarie Textiles Group, Moda Designs, Neoman, Solution 5, Sydney Neckwear and Top Ryde Tailoring.

Qantas and British Airways also announced plans in 1997 for the introduction of 'codesharing', where an aircraft of one airline carries its own flight number as well as that of the other airline on selected services. Qantas had already been operating in a similar way with more than a dozen other airlines around the world to open up new routes and offer increased services between destinations. The Qantas/British Airways codesharing proposal between regional centres in the United Kingdom, continental Europe and Australia was a logical development for their alliance, which would add eight destinations to the Qantas network and four to that of British Airways.

Under the arrangement, Qantas would codeshare on British Airways flights to five cities in the United Kingdom and three in Europe, while the British carrier would put its 'BA' flight designator on more than 70 codeshared Qantas flights around Australia.

Towards the end of a busy year, Qantas and British Airways announced plans to seek regulatory approval to codeshare on each other's services along the Kangaroo Route via south-east Asia. As a result of the proposed new alliance service passengers would be able to book on any of 82 services each week between Australia and London.

Including the existing regional services, the codeshare services on the Kangaroo Route would give business and leisure travellers the benefits of 'seamless' service on more than 310 flights each week between 18 destinations.

The proposed codesharing, new terminal operations in London and shared facilities—including the joint lounges—are logical developments in the relationship between Qantas and British Airways in the 1990s.

ABOVE: *Wunala Dreaming* at the Qantas Jet Base, Sydney.
BELOW: The distinctive tail featuring the Qantas kangaroo motif, well known throughout the world.

A SOLID BASE FOR THE FUTURE

Qantas—like British Airways a few years earlier—has responded positively to the discipline which privatisation brings, when government funding is replaced by private enterprise shareholder investment.

Under the leadership of the Board of Directors headed by chairman Gary Pemberton and an experienced senior management team led by chief executive James Strong, the airline has achieved the highest profitability and the fastest growth in its history during the past three financial years.

In August 1997, Qantas reported an operating profit before tax and abnormal items of $A420.9 million for the year to 30 June, up 4.9 per cent over the previous year. Passenger numbers for the 12 months reached a record 18.6 million, taking the growth for the three years up by more than 30 per cent. This was achieved with additional capacity of 25 per cent, reflecting more effective aircraft utilisation on both domestic and international operations. Staff levels and productivity also grew during the three years to the end of June 1997.

Mr Pemberton described the period as the strongest ever of business growth 'based on strategies of selective route development, priority investment in products and services and cost offsets from improved productivity and operating efficiency.'

The profit performance in a challenging economic and competitive environment, coupled with reductions in the company's cost structure and debt, have enabled a significant strengthening of the balance sheet. Operations on the Kangaroo Route have contributed to this growth.

ABOVE: Cockpit of the 747-400 illustrates the advances in flight instrumentation since the first Qantas flight to London.

Throughout the evolution of the Kangaroo Route, Qantas has continued its pioneering role in long-distance air travel. For as much as air travel has changed through its technical advances, travellers' needs have become no less exacting. In the 1930s, passengers aboard the flying boats appreciated the promenade deck and smoking room to withstand the 32-stop, nine-and-a-half-day flight between Sydney and London; in the 1940s, the Constellations introduced sleeper beds for First Class passengers.

THE WAY AHEAD

Playing a key role in the development of satellite-based navigation systems, the airline that once used roads and railways to find its way over the Queensland outback is now harnessing the latest satellite technology, opening up a new way to London. Deviating from the traditional route over India and the Middle East, Qantas is taking a leading role to inaugurate air corridors over western China and west over the northern skirts of the mighty Himalayas. The result will be a further saving in time, with up to 50 minutes likely to be shaved off the average flying time between South-East Asia and the United Kingdom.

The Kangaroo Route has been witness to, and has played a significant part in, political and aviation history. In the 50 years of flying 'the longest hop', Qantas has come full circle: it is once more privately owned, it is again flying within Australia, and British Airways and Qantas are once again partners on the Kangaroo Route.

ABOVE: Passengers on board a Super Constellation.
BELOW: The lounge area in the Super Constellation was popular on long flights.

super service at your command !

QANTAS

Roll of Honour

Lead Partners

Airservices Australia

Australian Air Express Pty Ltd

The Boeing Company

British Airways

John Singleton Advertising

Unisys Australia Ltd

Major Partners

Australia Post

Commonwealth Bank

Courtaulds Aerospace

Ford Motor Company of Australia Limited

Hertz Australia Pty Limited

Hewlett-Packard Australia Limited

ITT Sheraton Corporation

Lockheed Martin

Novotel Bangkok on Siam Square

PT. Jasa Angkasa Semesta

Singapore Airport Terminal Services

Australian Business Telephone Pty Ltd

Barnwell Cambridge Pty Ltd

SNP Security

General Partners

Airport Equipment Limited

Amdahl Australia Pty Ltd

Andersen Contracting

Attachmate Australasia Pty Ltd

Australian Federation of Travel Agents Ltd

Australian Petroleum Pty Ltd (Ampol)

Aviation Distributors Inc.

Bar Code Data Systems Pty Limited

BP Australia Limited

Broadlex Cleaning Australia Pty Limited

Brochure Flow International Limited

Capral Aluminium Limited

Caribiner Wavelength Pty Limited

Cathay Pacific Catering Services

Corporate Computer Sales (Australia) Pty Ltd

DynAir Ground Services Group

Glidepath Ltd

H H Robertson (Australia) Pty Limited

Holiday Tours & Travel Pte Ltd

KPMG

Memorex Telex Pty Limited

Mercadier Pty Ltd

Phoenix Contracting Pty Ltd

Polaris Communications

Rational Software Corporation Pty Ltd

SAS Institute Australia Pty Ltd

The Shell Company of Australia Limited

Siam Inter•Continental Bangkok

Telstra Corporation Limited

TFK Corporation

Thai Airports Ground Services Co., Ltd.

The Millennium Gloucester London

Trafalgar Tours

Turbine Overhaul Services Pte Ltd

The Westin Stamford and Westin Plaza

Qantas Wardrobe Partners

George Gross & Harry Who Design Company Pty Ltd

Calcoup Incorporated Pty Ltd

Ingwe Group Holdings Pty Limited

John Kaldor Fabricmaker Pty Limited

Kolotex Australia Pty Ltd

Luigi & Anthony Pty Ltd

Macquarie Textiles Group Ltd

Moda Designs Pty Ltd

Neoman Pty Ltd

Solution 5 Pty Limited

SF Corporate Clothing Pty Ltd

Sydney Neckwear Company Pty Ltd

Top Ryde Tailoring and Alterations Pty Ltd

The Qantas
GALLERY
of
EXCELLENCE

The story of Qantas is about the people with whom we work and who influence our customers' perceptions of what Qantas means to them.

One of the most important ingredients in determining our service mix is the quality of the products and services delivered to Qantas by our key supply partners.

The Qantas Gallery of Excellence recognises the contribution this important group of companies has made and how they have contributed to ensuring Qantas remains at the forefront of international aviation.

Airservices Australia

HEAD OFFICE
Alan Woods Building
25 Constitution Avenue
Canberra ACT 2601
PO Box 367
Canberra ACT 2601
Phone   (02) 6268 4111
Fax   (02) 6268 5683
Internet: www.airservices.gov.au

Chairman
          John Forsyth
*Chief Executive Officer and Managing
   Director*
          Bill Pollard

NEW SOUTH WALES
Prince Alfred Park Building
219–241 Cleveland Street
Strawberry Hills NSW 2012
Phone   (02) 9690 7111
Fax   (02) 9690 7121

SOUTH AUSTRALIA
Comcare Building
63 Pirie Street
Adelaide SA 5000
Phone   (08) 8205 7666
Fax   (08) 8205 7607

VICTORIA/TASMANIA
Level 1, 321 Exhibition Street
Melbourne VIC 3000
Phone   (03) 9339 2666
Fax   (03) 9667 8192

WESTERN AUSTRALIA
130 Fauntleroy Avenue
Redcliffe WA 6104
Phone   (08) 9476 8777
Fax   (08) 9476 8036

QUEENSLAND
Australia House, 363 Adelaide Street
Brisbane QLD 4000
Phone   (07) 3833 6211
Fax   (07) 3833 6311

(left to right)

The Flight Progress Board was used at major air traffic control centres between 1950 and 1967. It provided a means of recording the progress of flights, altitude assignment and the co-ordination of arrivals and departures. The advent of jet aircraft rendered this system obsolete, and it was superseded by radar control.

The Sydney Air Traffic Control Tower.

The Australian Advanced Air Traffic System (TAAATS) Centre in Brisbane. TAAATS will provide the first fully integrated air traffic control system for Australian airspace and will be one of the world's most advanced air traffic management systems.

An air traffic controller using TAAATS equipment.

Airservices' rescue and fire fighting service.

Airservices Australia is an airways services provider responsible for managing 11 per cent of the world's airspace. We are in the business of providing safe, efficient and effective air traffic management, and rescue and fire fighting services, to customers in the aviation industry.

Our principal services include:

- airspace management;
- air traffic control;
- traffic and flight information;
- navigation services;
- aeronautical information;
- aviation rescue and fire fighting;
- environmental regulation.

Airservices Australia's relationship with Qantas began more than a decade before the airline commenced operations on the Kangaroo Route.

In 1932, Airservices Australia's predecessor, the Civil Aviation Branch of the Department of Defence, held a position on an interdepartmental Government committee which investigated the development of air communications between Australia and the United Kingdom. At the time, it took 31 days for a letter from Sydney to reach London by the weekly mail steamer.

In 1934, the committee adopted an approach which developed an airlink from Australia to Singapore and provided an opportunity for Australia to operate for the first time in the international airmail business. Qantas was awarded the contract and continues to provide this service today.

From those early days to now, Airservices and Qantas have grown together. Today Qantas successfully operates in an increasingly competitive global air transport market and Airservices continues to respond to the air traffic needs of Qantas.

In this, the 50th anniversary of the Kangaroo Route, Airservices Australia salutes the achievements of Qantas and looks forward to our relationship continuing to provide safe and efficient operations between Australia and the United Kingdom, as well as in support of the many other routes into which Qantas has since expanded.

AIRSERVICES AUSTRALIA

Australian Air Express Pty Ltd

ACN 054 307 336

Level 2, 399 Elizabeth Street
Melbourne VIC 3000
PO Box 1324L
Melbourne VIC 3001

Phone: (03) 9297 3100
Fax: (03) 9297 3141
Internet: www.ausairx.com.au

Chairman: Graham John
Chief Executive, Australian air Express: Allen Buckley

Cnr Shiers Avenue and Fifth Street, Mascot NSW 2020
Phone: (02) 9582 1500 Fax: (02) 9582 1588

East Street, Melbourne Airport VIC 3043
Phone: (03) 9241 6500 Fax: (03) 9241 6550

Dryandra Road, Brisbane Airport QLD 4007
Phone: (07) 3874 7000 Fax: (07) 3874 7070

Arrival Road, Adelaide Airport SA 5950
Phone: (08) 8400 3500 Fax: (08) 8400 3540

Cnr Ross Drive and Boud Avenue, Perth Airport WA 6104
Phone: (08) 9231 8400 Fax: (08) 9231 8441

Sir Norman Brearley Drive, Darwin Airport NT 0810
Phone: (08) 8945 4074 Fax: (08) 8945 2778

Ulinga Place, Canberra Airport, Palligo ACT 2609
Phone: (02) 6200 3900 Fax: (02) 6200 3920

Cnr Long and Johnsons Street, Hobart Airport TAS 7170
Phone: (03) 6248 5660 Fax: (03) 6248 5538

Australian airExpress

NETWORK

Australian air Express (AaE) has Australia's largest and most powerful express freight network, operating the nation's only fully containerised air linehaul network from Cairns to Perth, including Hobart. More than 50 nightly inter-capital freighter flights are serviced by five jet aircraft, with charter facilities also available. Complementing this freighter service is the exclusive access to the locker space on more than 250 Qantas passengers flights per day. On the ground an extensive linehaul fleet of more than 350 radio-controlled courier vehicles operate a network poised to deliver true overnight service to virtually all post code areas in the country. Augmenting AaE's air and road networks, customers have unique access to Australia Post Corporation's vast network of post offices and agencies, which includes delivery to PO boxes. With more than 40 depots in Australia, AaE provides a truly national door-to-door express parcel pick-up and delivery service.

TECHNOLOGY

The company is aware of the influence that technological change brings when relating with clients. AaE has upgraded the track and trace capability with new laser scanning technology and was the first Australian company to introduce Internet-based track and trace facilities. In conjunction with these initiatives, a significant investment has been made to the company's overall telecommunications equipment, providing all the call centres and offices with new communications equipment.

The company has an ongoing commitment to continuous refinement and progressive development of technologies which provide greater levels of customer service and generate efficiencies throughout the organisation.

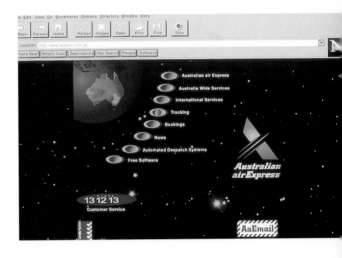

SERVICES

All consignments are bar coded for computerised tracking and signed for on delivery—with full insurance options.

Next Flight	- pick-up and delivery on the same day
Overnight	- delivery AM next business day (including prepaid satchels) to major cities
Next Day	- delivery PM next business day
Off Peak	- delivery time within 72 hours
Perishables	- airport to airport service; coolrooms available.

The Boeing Company

ARBN 002 590 285

PO Box 3707
Seattle WA 98124-2207
USA

Phone: (1) 425 237 2121
Fax: (1) 425 237 7270

Internet: www.boeing.com

President BCAG
Ron Woodard
Vice-President International Sales
Seddik Belyamani

Boeing International Corporation
Level 3, 15 Bourke Road
Mascot NSW 2020

Sales Director Australia & Pacific Islands
G L Soholt

Partners for the Long Haul

When Qantas ordered its first Boeing airliner back in 1956, the two companies established a truly long-haul partnership. More than 41 years later, Qantas has now taken delivery of 164 Boeing jets. These jets have always been front-line performers on the key Kangaroo Route.

Boeing aircraft have helped Qantas meet the competition and ongoing passenger demand for performance and comfort on one of the world's toughest air routes.

Because the Qantas mission has always involved conquering the tyranny of distance, the Australian airline's long-haul expertise has continually attracted respect from Seattle. As the airline industry required greater payload and range, Qantas became a key contributor to Boeing developments to meet these needs.

In contrast to the early Qantas Boeing 707s which flew multi-stop services from Australia to London, today's 747-400 flagships handle the route in daily single-stop comfort. The airline's 1989 record-setting London–Sydney non-stop flight was an impressive combination of Qantas experience and 747-400 performance.

More recently, the best-selling Boeing 737 has been the mainstay of the strong domestic presence of Qantas, with two models of the versatile Boeing 767, the -200ER and -300ER, offering the right mix of capacity and range for both local and regional routes.

Boeing was honoured to win the Qantas 'Engineering and Maintenance' supplier of the year award in 1996, reflecting the effort we've put into building our relationship.

Around the world, Boeing airliners have carried more than 13 billion passengers, and more than half the jetliners ever built have been Boeings. This success has been achieved by working together with pace-setting airlines such as Qantas.

Boeing is proud to have been an integral part of the Qantas success story. And as the Qantas mission demands further aircraft improvements, Boeing will be there working together with Qantas to meet aviation's future challenges.

BRITISH AIRWAYS

BRITISH AIRWAYS—A LEADER IN AVIATION

British Airways has a long and proud history of pioneering development in aviation.

Born in 1924 as Imperial Airways, the airline was charged with building a worldwide system to link the scattered peoples of the then British Empire.

British Airways and its predecessors operated the world's first daily scheduled international air service, the world's first jet passenger flight and the world's first commercial supersonic aircraft.

From its earliest days the carrier had a co-operative relationship with Qantas to promote travel and communication between Australia and Britain. Imperial Airways was an early shareholder in Qantas Empire Airways.

In 1934 they jointly opened the route between Britain and Australia: Imperial Airways flew between London and Singapore and Qantas between Singapore and Australia. The trip took 12 days.

As BOAC, and subsequently as British Airways, the airline has operated services in its own right between Britain and Australia since 1948.

A Boeing 747–400 with a world image from Poland by Dunta Wojda. It is one of 50 World Images commissioned by the airline as part of its new identity.

BRITISH AIRWAYS—THE NEW AIRLINE FOR THE NEW MILLENNIUM

1997 marked the launch of a new strategic direction and a radical new identity for the world's most profitable airline, backed by a £6 billion three-year program of investment in new services, products, aircraft facilities and training.

The goal of the airline's new direction has been to establish British Airways as the undisputed leader in world travel as it flies into the 21st century.

British Airways is presented as an airline of the world, born and based in Britain, but passionately committed to serving and connecting the communities of the world.

The new corporate identity is the 'visual promise' of the many improvements that will flow for customers from the company's repositioning.

Fifty world images, which include the Aboriginal inspired designs *Wunala Dreaming* and *Nalanji Dreaming* (originally created for two Qantas 747 aircraft in 1994) will appear on the tails of its 308 aircraft and thousands of items from ground vehicles to tickets.

Sky-High Meeting: British Airway's revolutionary new FIRST service for premium passengers provides every passenger with an individual compartment that can be used for business meetings or dinner for two and then convert to a full flat flying bed.

QANTAS AND BRITISH AIRWAYS—A BRILLIANT PARTNERSHIP

With 244 destinations in 66 countries and a choice of 18 stopovers, customers need not waste time wondering where British Airways and Qantas fly, but rather, where they don't.

The alliance between these two leading airlines of the world was announced by the Australian Government in December 1992 and formalised when British Airways completed its $665 million investment in Qantas in March 1993.

It has resulted in significant improvements in service for customers of both carriers, including a greater choice of business and leisure stopover fares; reciprocity between frequent flyer programs* and airport lounges; and, most importantly, a much greater choice of flights per week from Australia to Europe.

*not available all markets

A Boeing 747–400 high in the skies, with a Celtic World Image by Timothy O'Neill

Level 26 AIDC Tower
201 Kent Street
Sydney NSW 2000

Phone: (02) 9258 3200
Fax: (02) 9258 3285

Internet: www.BRITISH-AIRWAYS.com

General Manager: Nick Tait
Regional Manager South-West Pacific: Neil Harrison

ACN 002 747 597

John Singleton Advertising
(Aust) Pty Limited

ACN 003 326 609

Level 18
201 Sussex Street
Sydney NSW 2000

Phone: (02) 9373 6333
Fax: (02) 9373 6399

E-mail: info@jsa.com.au
Internet: www.jsa.com.au

Chief Executive Officer: John Singleton
Managing Director: Russell Tate

208–212 Park Street
South Melbourne VIC 3205

7 Marie Street
Milton QLD 4064

SINGLETON
ADVERTISING

John Singleton Advertising is the largest wholly Australian-owned agency and ranks within the top 10 agencies nationally. As a wholly owned subsidiary of Singleton Group Limited, it is the only publicly listed advertising agency in Australia.

From its formation in 1985, the agency has achieved consistent and spectacular growth. Since 1991 billings have increased from $40 million to over $160 million per annum.

The agency's philosophy is a very simple one—advertising exists to sell! And fundamental to our ability to 'sell' our clients' products is the need to preserve and evolve the integrity of their brands.

Our client list includes some of the great brand names in Australia and we are especially proud of our association with Qantas, by any measure one of the greatest Australian brands of all.

Unisys Australia Limited

ARBN 000 002 086

WORLD HEADQUARTERS
Unisys Corporation
Township Line and Union Meeting Roads
Blue Bell
Pennsylvania 19424 USA

Phone: (1) 215 986 4011
Fax: (1) 215 986 6004
Internet: www.unisys.com

HEAD OFFICE AUSTRALIA
Unisys Australia Limited
213 Miller Street
North Sydney NSW 2060
Phone: (02) 9931 6666
Fax: (02) 9957 3370

574 St Kilda Road Melbourne VIC 3004
Phone: (03) 9522 3666 Fax: (03) 9522 3674

91 Northbourne Avenue Turner ACT 2601
Phone: (02) 6274 3555 Fax: (02) 6274 3533

147 Coronation Drive Milton QLD 4064
Phone: (07) 3361 1888 Fax: (07) 3361 1866

10 Kingspark Rd West Perth WA 6005
Phone: (08) 9481 0577 Fax: (08) 9321 4426

Unisys is an information management company—we help our clients transform their business by creating innovative solutions that change the way they use information. Our clients include many of the world's largest financial services companies, leading communications companies, major airlines and transportation companies, and government agencies.

Our relationship with Qantas spans almost a quarter of a century. In the 1970s we worked closely with Australian Airlines and a number of international airlines to develop a reservation system which became the basis of our USAS airlines application suite.

During the following decade, we developed departure control, maintenance, engineering and flight operations systems with Australian Airlines and the USAS Freight Management applications with Qantas. More recently, we have developed and delivered advanced revenue management and airport processing systems in partnership with Qantas Airways.

Our association with Qantas has substantially contributed to the development of a comprehensive suite of airline and travel application systems now employed by over 150 of the world's airlines.

In addition, we have provided Qantas with the advanced technology to run these applications—from the first Univac 494 Dual Processor in 1971 to the Unisys 2200/900 in 1995 and in 1997 with ClearPath. Qantas continues to employ our most advanced and powerful computing technology.

Qantas is an important Unisys customer. We have greatly enjoyed working with Qantas, delivering information systems to enhance its position as one of the world's leading airlines.

We congratulate Qantas on 50 years of service on the Kangaroo Route.

GEORGE GROSS AND HARRY WHO DESIGN COMPANY PTY LTD
ACN 008 074 744

214 Gilbert Street, Adelaide SA 5000, Phone: (08) 8212 2295 Fax: (08) 8231 1291
Trade Name: *George Gross, Harry Who, G2*
Managing Director: George Gross, Director: Harry Watt

Designers to Qantas.

CALCOUP INCORPORATED PTY LIMITED
ACN 003 449 269

15 Harp Street, Belmore NSW 2192
PO Box 204, Belmore NSW 2192
Phone: (02) 9718 7377 Fax: (02) 9718 7482
Trade Name: *Calcoup Knitwear*
Managing Director: Neil Couper
Director: Peter Callaghan

Manufacturers of quality knitted garments using Australian wool for the uniform and leisure markets.

KOLOTEX AUSTRALIA PTY LTD
ACN 002 716 716

22 George Street, Leichhardt NSW 2040
PO Box 71, Leichhardt NSW 2040
Phone: (02) 9335 2900 Fax: (02) 9551 9115
Trade Name: *Sheer Relief*
Chief Executive Officer: Clive Sacher
Group Marketing Manager: Graham Newman

Kolotex is proud to supply Sheer Relief hosiery to Qantas for their uniform requirements since 1972.
All-day support: all-day comfort.

INGWE GROUP HOLDINGS PTY LIMITED
ACN 001 448 488

13 Hordern Place, Camperdown NSW 2050
PO Box 630, Strawberry Hills NSW 2012
Phone: (02) 9517 9666 Fax: (02) 9516 4400
Trade Name: *Ingwe Masasa Impi*
E-mail: ingwe@itlite.com.au
Internet: www.masasa.com.au
Chairman: Malcolm Holland
Managing Director: Andrew Holland

Speciality buttons, badges, buckles, labels and other garment trimmings plus imaginative corporate gifts, promotional items and floral arrangements of the highest quality.

LUIGI & ANTHONY PTY LTD
ACN 001 117 942

117 Constitution Road, Dulwich Hill NSW 2203
PO Box 61, Dulwich Hill NSW 2203
Phone: (02) 9550 9255 Fax: (02) 9550 9343
Managing Director: Luigi Alibrandi
Managing Director: Anthony Alibrandi

Since its inception in 1964, Luigi & Anthony Pty Ltd has represented a synergy of Italian craftsmanship and Australian ingenuity. We are proud to have been associated with Qantas for the last 12 years, supplying the uniform with quality, Australian-made men's trousers and shorts, and ladies' skirts and slacks.

JOHN KALDOR

JOHN KALDOR FABRICMAKER PTY LIMITED
ACN 000 142 307
110 McEvoy Street
Alexandria NSW 2014
Phone: (02) 9698 7700 Fax: (02) 9698 1375
Chief Executive: John Kaldor, AM

John Kaldor sells apparel and decorative fabrics to the international market. John Kaldor is proud to supply the Qantas uniform with the 'Cosmic Blue' corporate print and the 'Cosmic Blue' plain chambray as well as the white shirting fabric. John Kaldor is also very pleased that they are now supplying the most recent addition to the Qantas uniform for flight attendants, the 'Wattle' jacquard.

MACQUARIE TEXTILES GROUP LTD
ACN 000 012 877

Bridge Street, Albury NSW 2640
PO Box 319, Albury NSW 2640
Phone: (02) 6043 0200 Fax: (02) 6041 1321
Trade Name: *Macquarie Textiles*
Managing Director: John Lewis
Chairman: Merv Collens

The Macquarie Group is Australia's largest woollen and worsted textile company.
Macquarie produces an impressive range of woollen and worsted fabrics for apparel, furnishing and blanketing.

McHUGH ENTERPRISES PTY LTD

ACN 072 025 640

212–220 Parramatta Road, Camperdown NSW 2050
PO Box 397, Camperdown NSW 2050
Phone: (02) 9516 2811 Fax: (02) 9550 5117
Trade Name: *Moda Designs*
Managing Director: Lindsay McHugh
Chief Designer: Frank Gilio

Moda Designs, makers of distinctive corporate fashion, have been Sydney's largest CMT manufacturer of uniforms and suiting due to excellence of service and quality, for the last 27 years.

NEOMAN PTY LTD

ACN 001 666 217

172–182 Princes Highway, Arncliffe NSW 2205
PO Box 172, Arncliffe NSW 2205
Phone: (02) 9567 7700 Fax: (02) 9567 2555
Trade Names: *Country Road Clothing, Rainer, Messini Disimor, Rarity Shirts, Gowing Bros Ltd.*
Managing Director: Gunter H Zechner
Director: Juana E Zechner

Neoman have been successfully servicing our most demanding clientele for over 25 years. We are recognised for uncompromising reliability and quality standards beyond Australia's borders.
Neoman means quality.

SOLUTION 5

SOLUTION 5 PTY LIMITED

ACN 003 770 910

Unit 1/263 Alfred Street, North Sydney NSW 2060
Phone: (02) 9929 6644 Fax: (02) 9929 6655
E-mail: solvinfo@solvit.com.au
Internet: www.solvit.com.au
Managing Director: Satis Patel
Finance Director: Pankaj Patel

Solution 5 supplies luggage, leather belts and accessories for the Qantas uniform, as well as Qantas Frequent Flyer cabin bags and small leathergoods.

SF CORPORATE CLOTHING PTY LTD

ACN 054 692 901

76–82 Botany Road, Alexandria NSW 2015
PO Box 156, Alexandria NSW 2015
Phone: (02) 9310 7000 Fax: (02) 9310 7111
E-mail: dgrundy@ibm.com.au
Managing Director: David Grundy

SF Corporate Clothing, Australia's leading manufacturer and supplier of high-quality corporate clothing, is committed to providing their customers with a product that promotes the highest levels of comfort, style and professionalism.

SYDNEY NECKWEAR COMPANY PTY LTD

ACN 003 876 819

221–229 Sydney Park Road, Erskineville NSW 2043
PO Box 161, Erskineville NSW 2043
Phone: (02) 9565 1811 Fax: (02) 9565 1075
Trade Names: *John & Lois Ties*
Joint Managing Director: Philip Zylstra
Joint Managing Director: David Zylstra

The Sydney Neckwear Company has supplied Qantas with quality neckwear for the last 12 years. We are the leading supplier of corporate neckwear throughout Australia.

TOP RYDE TAILORING AND ALTERATIONS PTY LTD

ACN 002 672 737

95 Blaxland Road, Ryde NSW 2112
Phone: (02) 9809 2642 Fax: (02) 9809 7935
Chairman: Sam Olivieri
Managing Director: Frank Olivieri

Top Ryde Tailoring and Alterations has a staff of 14 fully qualified tailors and machinists able to handle all aspects of ladies' and gents' alterations as well as men's tailoring.

Australia Post

321 Exhibition Street
Melbourne VIC 3000
GPO Box 1777Q
Melbourne VIC 3001
Phone: (03) 9204 7171
Fax: (03) 9663 1160
Internet: www.auspost.com.au

Chairman: Linda Nicholls
Managing Director: Graeme John

Australia Post is one of Australia's strongest performing corporations and one of the world's foremost postal services.

Since corporatisation in 1989, Post has transformed its culture and lifted its financial performance to become one of Australia's most successful businesses. On every financial and operational measure, Australia Post's performance today is the best it has ever been.

A key aspect of this performance is the reliability of mail deliveries. Over the past year Australia Post has delivered 93.9 per cent of domestic standard letters on time or earlier. This is a world leading performance and was achieved while mail volumes for the year increased by over four per cent to 4.2 billion items.

The cost of sending mail in Australia is among the lowest in the world, with a domestic standard letter rate of 45 cents. The rate has remained unchanged since January 1992, reducing the real cost by over five cents per letter.

Australia Post runs Australia's largest retail network, serving 800,000 customers every day with some 300 million transactions handled every year. It also operates the largest over-the-counter bill payment service in the country. Through giroPost, customers also have access to 'on-line' services with 10 banks and financial institutions at more than 2,600 postal outlets across the country.

Australia Post —dedicated to providing innovative and easy-to-use products, friendly service and consistent on-time delivery at the lowest achievable cost.

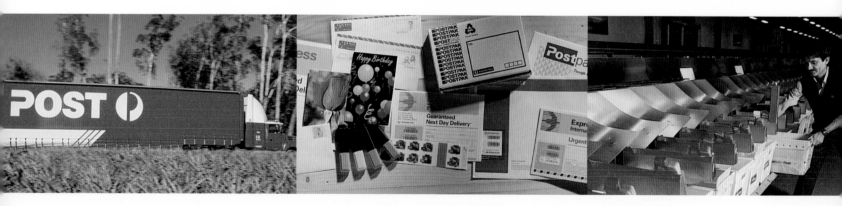

Commonwealth Bank

Commonwealth Bank of Australia ACN 123 123 124

48 Martin Place
Sydney NSW 2000
GPO Box 2719, Sydney NSW 1155
Phone: (02) 9378 2000
Fax: (02) 9378 3668
Internet: www.commbank.com.au

Managing Director: David Murray
General Manager, Personal Banking: Alf Long

Qantas and the Commonwealth Bank—meeting the needs of all Australians.

Qantas has a history of being committed to meeting the aviation needs of all Australians. Just as we at the Commonwealth Bank have always been committed to meeting the banking and financial services needs of all our customers across Australia, including Qantas. We have acted on behalf of Qantas to meet its varying banking needs for almost 80 years. From being involved with the leasing of aircraft, to the development of innovative and cost-effective financial packages, and assisting Qantas with the redevelopment of its Sydney Domestic Terminal.

We offer a variety of products, services and programs to meet the varied needs of all our business and personal customers. Also, being the largest issuer of credit cards in Australia, it's not surprising that we have a number of unique initiatives in this area. One of the more innovative products available for business customers is the Commonwealth Bank Business Card. This is an all-in-one business credit card that combines the features of a corporate card (travel and entertainment) and a purchasing card (day-to-day business purchases). Believed to be a world first, this card eliminates the need to have different commercial cards within the one organisation. If you would like further details, please call our Business Line on 13 19 98 (8am–8pm, Monday to Friday).

Another successful initiative by the Bank is the True Awards loyalty program. Personal customers can earn valuable award points simply by paying with their Commonwealth Bank credit card with the up to 55 days' interest free option and then redeem awards such as shopping, entertainment, travel, plus special banking awards. Members can even use their points to donate towards a charity. For further details, please call our True Awards Service Centre on 131 661 (8am–8pm, Monday to Friday).

We are proud to be associated with Qantas, a company which, like the Commonwealth Bank, is committed to looking after the needs of all Australians—now and in the future.

COURTAULDS AEROSPACE

ACN 050 106 217

Courtaulds Aerospace Australia
23 Ovata Drive
Tullamarine VIC 3043

Phone: (03) 9335 1557
Fax: (03) 9335 3490
E-mail: robert.barry@courtaulds.com.au

Contacts: Robert Barry, Anne Neeson

Recognised by Qantas as the world leader in aerospace coatings, sealants and packaging technology.
Now offering Qantas and airlines worldwide our new generation topcoat.

Desothane®HS

* Excellent application properties
* Maximises UV resistance and gloss retention
* Extends service life
* Complies with global VOC regulations

Courtaulds Aerospace UK
Phone: +44 1388 772541
Fax: +44 1388 774373
Contact: David Hughes

Courtaulds Aerospace USA
Phone: +1 818 240 2060
Fax: +1 818 549 7595
Contact: Randy Cameron

Courtaulds Coatings South Africa
Phone: +27 (0) 11 907 8195
Fax: +27 (0) 11 907 2316
Contact: Roald Johannsen

Courtaulds Aerospace France
Phone: +33 (0) 2 3553 5400
Fax: +33 (0) 2 3443 5405
Contact: Patrice Bibring

Courtaulds Aerospace Hong Kong
Phone: +852 2827 7883
Fax: +852 2827 9117/9488
Contact: Tony Chan

Courtaulds Aerospace Saudi Arabia
Phone: +966 (0) 3 842 8436
Fax: +966 (0) 3 842 4361
Contact: Karl Berger

Courtaulds Aerospace Germany
Phone: +49 (0) 40 720030
Fax: +49 (0) 40 7208268
Contact: Uli Wesolowski

Courtaulds Aerospace Singapore
Phone: +65 861 1119
Fax: +65 861 6162
Contact: Jet Shyang Tan

Desothane®HS is a registered trademark of Courtaulds Aerospace Inc.

THE LONGEST HOP

Ford Motor Company
of Australia Limited

ACN 004 116 223

1735 Sydney Road
Campbellfield VIC 3061
Private Bag 6
Campbellfield VIC 3061
Phone: (03) 9359 8211
Fax: (03) 9359 8200
Internet: www.ford.com.au

President: David Morgan

Central Region—8 Greenhill Road, Wayville SA 5034. Phone: (08) 8372 5799 Fax: (08) 8373 1251
Western Region—Level 2, 1100 Hay Street, West Perth WA 6005. Phone: (08) 9320 7444 Fax: (08) 9320 7400
Northern Region—175 Melbourne Street, South Brisbane QLD 4101. Phone: (07) 3332 1299 Fax: (07) 3844 5866
Eastern Region—Building 1, Level 2, Pymble Corporate Centre, 20 Bridge Street, Pymble NSW 2073. Phone: (02) 9488 1177 Fax: (02) 9488 1188

Ford's total investment in Australia, at $1.05 billion, is the largest of all local vehicle producers in Australia.
Ford has been overall market leader 11 times (1982–90 and 1995–96) in the last 16 years, and is still market leader to date. Falcon is the nation's top-selling car.
Over one in every five new passengers cars currently sold in Australia is a Ford.
There are more Ford vehicles on Australian roads than any other marque.
Total vehicle production in 1996 totalled 103,659, comprising 92,493 passenger cars (Falcon, Fairmont, Fairlane and LTD), 10,231 Falcon utilities/vans, and 935 trucks (Trader and Louisville).
Ford Australia currently employs nearly 6,300 people in its operations in Geelong and Broadmeadows in Victoria, and Brisbane in Queensland, as well as in its five regional offices in each mainland capital city.

Hertz Australia Pty Limited

ACN 004 407 087

Level 6, 10 Dorcas Street
South Melbourne VIC 3205
PO Box 181
South Melbourne VIC 3205
Phone: (03) 9698 2444
Fax: (03) 9698 3561

Managing Director: James Bowyer

In 1918, in Chicago, Hertz invented the car rental business.

Today, Hertz is the largest and number one car rental company in the world. It has been for almost 80 years. In fact, Hertz has over 5,400 rental locations in 150 countries, including over 230 locations around Australia.

Hertz offers a wide range of the largest model vehicles, from small and economy size vehicles, family sedans and station wagons, luxury vehicles, four-wheel drives, campervans, mini buses, light commercials and trucks.

Hertz is committed to continuing to be the industry innovator, and to providing the very best of service, at competitive rates, to both business and leisure renters alike, who appreciate the convenience and flexibility that only car rental offers.

Hewlett-Packard Australia Limited

ACN 004 394 763

31–41 Joseph Street
Blackburn VIC 3130
PO Box 221, Blackburn VIC 3130
Phone: (03) 9272 2895
Fax: (03) 9898 7831
Internet: www.hp.com

Chief Executive Officer: Bruce Thompson
Director of Personnel and Quality: Hans Nièlson

'Offices on the Park', 8 Greenhill Road, Wayville SA 5034
Phone: (08) 8229 3910 Fax: (08) 8357 9589

50 McDougall Street, Milton QLD 4064
Phone: (07) 3858 2222 Fax: (07) 3369 6280

Thynne Street, Fern Hill Park, Bruce ACT 2617
Phone: (02) 6274 3600 Fax: (02) 6251 6948

Herdsman Business Park, 66 Hasler Road, Osborne Park WA 6017
Phone: (08) 9441 8000   Fax: (08) 9242 1682

17–23 Talavera Road, North Ryde NSW 2113
Phone: (02) 9950 7444   Fax: (02) 9888 9072

Hewlett-Packard (HP) is the world's second largest IT corporation. Its massive portfolio of hardware, middleware, software and services extends into the business, technical, industrial and personal computing markets.

HP's products include numerous industry standards such as its HP9000 Unix computing hardware and OpenView middleware, as well as household names such as its LaserJet printers. Services include systems administration and network management, implementation, project management, testing and measurement, education and training.

The company has 120,500 employees worldwide and recorded revenues of US$38.4 billion in its 1996 fiscal year. For the same year, its Australian and New Zealand revenues grew 22 per cent to $880 million.

Qantas first deployed HP's OpenView network management system to assist in the global rollout of QUBE, its state-of-the-art booking and reservations system. It uses HP OpenView to manage its entire TCP/IP network across its dozens of offices around the world. The network comprises around 12,000 devices at present, but by the Year 2000 this is expected to grow to around 50,000. The entire OpenView system runs on several dedicated HP network management workstations located in the main offices of Qantas in Sydney and Melbourne.

THE LUXURY COLLECTION℠

ITT SHERATON

Sheraton
HOTELS & RESORTS

ITT Sheraton
Club International

ITT Sheraton Corporation

ACN 000 575 048

Level 15, 179 Elizabeth Street
Sydney NSW 2000
PO Box A242, Sydney South NSW 1235
Phone: (02) 9373 3100
Fax: (02) 9373 3171
Internet: www.sheraton.com

President, Asia–Pacific Division: Ed Davie
Vice President, Director of Sales & Marketing, Asia–Pacific Division: Steve Nikolov

For many years along the Kangaroo Route, Qantas and ITT Sheraton have shared not only similar values of quality and service, but many of the same customers.

Which is perhaps one reason that today, almost everywhere that Qantas flies, ITT Sheraton has a hotel or resort. As Qantas expands its presence in the Asia–Pacific region, ITT Sheraton will continue to be there for Qantas passengers, doubling the number of properties in the region over the next few years.

ITT Sheraton is proud to enjoy a close working relationship with Qantas, through the co-operation of the ITT Sheraton Club International and Qantas Frequent Flyer program.

Congratulations on 50 great years, Qantas. We look forward to many more years of fruitful partnership.

Lockheed Martin

103 Chesapeake Park Plaza
Baltimore MD 21220 USA
Phone: (1) 410 682 1210
Fax: (1) 410 682 1112

Vice President and General Manager: J Raymond Roquemore
Director of Customer Support: Charles M Schaeffer

When the Lockheed Constellation flew the first Kangaroo Route in 1947, the Lockheed and Martin heritage companies already had more than 30 years of experience designing and building aircraft. Fifty years later, Lockheed Martin enjoys a rich aeronautics heritage unparalleled by any company in the industry. True to the spirit of aviation's earliest pioneers, Lockheed Martin continues to build on this foundation. Today Lockheed Martin companies are setting the standard for designing, building and servicing aircraft the world over.

One of those companies, located on the site of the original Martin Aircraft Company, is the Lockheed Martin Center for Aircraft Maintenance (CAM). The CAM provides the high quality and quick response today's customers need on overhauls and repairs for large engine thrust reversers and aerostructures.

As an original aerostructure manufacturer, the CAM provides OEM-quality repair and parts in our 1.6 million square foot facility. An FAA/JAA certified full service station, CAM is staffed with trained AP mechanics, seasoned aerostructures, professionals and quality engineers.

The CAM, together with Lockheed Martin companies worldwide, salute the Qantas heritage; its service to the air travel industry and its continuance of the pioneering spirit.

Novotel Bangkok
on Siam Square

ACN 1520 585 744

Siam Square SOI 6
Phatumwan, Bangkok 10330
THAILAND
Phone: (66) 2 255 6888
Fax: (66) 2 255 1824
E-mail: novotel@ksc.th.com
Internet: www.hotelweb.fr

General Manager: Oswald Pichler
Director of Sales and Marketing: Christine Woo

Novotel Bangkok on Siam Square is truly the heart and soul of Bangkok. Enjoy panoramic views across Bangkok from our elegantly appointed guest rooms and suites, then take time to explore our breathtaking choice of gourmet dining options, all of which offer outstanding quality and fine service. Unwind a little and relax by the pool, work out in the fitness centre or, if business calls, rely on the comprehensive services of our business centre and meetings and conference facilities. After dark, head for Concept CM Square, the hotel's pulsing and exciting entertainment complex which is the heartbeat of Bangkok nightlife. All this, right in the heart and soul of Bangkok, with the shopping district of Siam Square at your doorstep.

For business or leisure travel, choose Novotel Bangkok on Siam Square, right at the heart and soul of Bangkok.

We know you'll feel at home right away. After all, we're the business class of hotels.

PT. Jasa Angkasa Semesta

ACN 005 956 011 (American Express Bank)

7th Floor, Suite 706, Lippo Life Building
Jl H R Rasuna Said Kav B 10–11
Jakarta 12910
INDONESIA
Phone: (62) 21 520 0322, 525 0988, 252 0870, 520 0303
Fax: (62) 21 520 7853
E-mail: usr20027@indosat.net.id

President Director: Sutoyo
Vice President Director: Arifin Sarodji

Terminal D, Room DOP 48–50
Soekarno – Hatta Airport, Jakarta
Phone: (6221) 550 7397, 550 7390
Fax: (6221) 550 1808, 550 1591
Sita: CGKAPXH

International Departure Check-in Hall
Ngurah Rai International Airport, Bali
Phone: (62361) 75 5542, 75 2949/59
Fax: (62361) 75 2307
Sita: DPSAPXH

Room 10, Airlines Office Building
Juanda Airport, Surabaya
Phone: (6231) 866 7751, 866 7635
Fax: (6231) 866 7643
Sita: SUBAPXH

Office Building Sam Ratulangi Airport, Manado
Phone: (62431) 81 2056, 86 0449 Ext. 183, 184
Fax: (62431) 81 2056

Kantor Cabang Bandara Hasanuddin
Ujung Pandang, Sulawesi Selatan
Phone: (62411) 51 4238
Fax: (62411) 51 3820

Excellent service in the air comes from professional ground handling.

Singapore Airport Terminal Services

55, Airport Boulevard
Singapore Changi Airport
SINGAPORE 819647
Phone: (65) 541 8100
Fax: (65) 543 2063

Chief Executive SATS Airport Services: Tan Hui Boon
Chief Executive SATS Catering: Yap Kim Wah

SATS congratulates Qantas Airways on the 50th anniversary of the Qantas Kangaroo Route.

We are proud to be associated with Qantas Airways on this momentous occasion.

We have 50 years of ground handling experience. Our range of comprehensive services includes apron handling, cargo handling, passenger services, catering, aircraft interior cleaning, security services, technical ramp handling and flight operations services.

ЭIRPORT ЭQUIPMENT LTD AIRPORT EQUIPMENT LIMITED

2–14 Rutherford Street
Lower Hutt
New Zealand
PO Box 30087 Lower Hutt

Phone   (64) 4 566 3574
Fax   (64) 4 569 3230

E-mail   aequip@xtra.co.nz

Managing Director
          Duncan McLennan
Workshop Manager
          Colin McLennan

Airport Equipment Limited was established in 1974 as a manufacturer of ground support equipment for the airline industry, and to specialise in the construction of Aircraft Passenger Boarding Bridges through an association with Jetway Systems of the United States.

To date, over 100 units have been installed and are in all major airports in the South Pacific area.

Airport Equipment Limited offers experience and expertise in the planning of apron layouts, the supply and installation of operationally proven products, and provides extensive after sales service and support for clients.

Airport Equipment Limited appreciate the relationship with Qantas Airways in working together to provide better and more advanced passenger handling facilities, and congratulate them on achieving the 50th anniversary of the Kangaroo Route.

amdahl

AMDAHL AUSTRALIA PTY LTD

ACN 002 533 342

Level 7
155 George Street
Sydney NSW 2000
PO Box N128
Grosvenor Place NSW 1220

Phone   (02) 9561 9999
Fax   (02) 9561 9811

Internet   www.amdahl.com

Vice President and General Manager
          Robert Hogg
Director, Marketing Operations
          Tom Langley

Amdahl provides integrated enterprise computing solutions designed to meet the demanding requirements of the world's most computer-intensive environments. Amdahl combines proprietary products and services with best-of-breed, third-party offerings, creating customised solutions that give customers a competitive advantage in their industries. Amdahl offerings include large-scale System/390 compatible processors, enterprise servers, data storage subsystems, and highly advanced software for systems and application management and applications development. Amdahl and its subsidiaries also provide a full range of professional and operational consulting services.

With more than 10,000 employees worldwide, Amdahl's products and services are available in over 30 countries. In the Asia–Pacific region, Amdahl has operations in Australia, New Zealand, Hong Kong, China, Malaysia, Singapore, Thailand, Korea and Indonesia.

ANDERSEN CONTRACTING

ANDERSEN SOFTWARE SERVICES PTY LTD
TRADING AS ANDERSEN CONTRACTING

ACN 003 366 783

141 Walker Street
North Sydney NSW 2060

Phone	(02) 9927 5400
Fax	(02) 9964 9767

E-mail	sheryle.a.moon@ac.com
Internet	www.swcontracting.com.au

Managing Partner
    Sheryle Moon
Senior Manager
    Melanie Kontze

360 Elizabeth Street, Melbourne VIC 3000
Phone: (03) 9286 7001 Fax: (03) 9286 7522

12 Creek Street, Brisbane QLD 4000
Phone: (07) 3309 4466 Fax: (07) 3309 4477

45 Johnstone Street, Wellington, New Zealand
Phone: (64) 4 471 1530 Fax: (64) 4 471 1585

Andersen Contracting designs flexible workforce solutions for any IT&T project.

To meet accelerating changes, enterprises today are becoming nimble, harnessing more resources and increasing their responsiveness to the marketplace. One element of this is the virtual workforce—where a fluid, flexible pool of resources can be drawn upon.

Our relationship with Qantas began over 18 months ago. Working with Qantas has allowed us to understand its workplace needs and propose a variable workforce solution to simplify and streamline the resourcing and acquisition process to satisfy the IT&T resourcing objectives at Qantas.

We offer the processes and skills to assist you in preparing for tomorrow's workplace. The outcome is a competitive edge involving a flexible environment conducive to the changing nature of workplaces and the global economy.

Andersen Contracting is a separate business organisation within Andersen Consulting.

Attachmate ™

ATTACHMATE AUSTRALASIA PTY LTD

ACN 005 511 517

Level 2, 77 Southbank Boulevard
South Melbourne VIC 3205

Phone	(03) 9694 6711
Fax	(03) 9686 9036

E-mail	aus-info@attachmate.com
Internet	www.attachmate.com

Area Manager—Australia/New Zealand
    Eddie J Baghdikian
Finance Director
    Keith Bold

Level 3, 20 Rodborough Road, Frenchs Forest NSW 2086
Phone: (02) 9975 7188 Fax: (02) 9415 4034

Attachmate is the leading supplier of information access software and services to major corporations, large organisations and government agencies worldwide. The company's connectivity solutions—object-oriented client and server software, authoring tools, management software, and hardware—safely extend enterprise systems, applications and data to end user customers.

Attachmate software is installed in over 95 per cent of the world's airlines and our continued focus on this industry has resulted in the customisation of products to meet an airline's specific integration and printing needs.

Attachmate has been developing and marketing products since 1982, providing industry leadership, innovation and outstanding support and service to over ten million users.

For more information about Attachmate's products, contact Attachmate's headquarters in Bellevue, Washington at (1) 425 644 4010, (1) 425 747 9924 (fax) or toll free at (800) 426 6283.

AUSTRALIAN FEDERATION OF TRAVEL AGENTS LTD

ACN 001 444 275
Level 3, 309 Pitt Street
Sydney NSW 2000

Phone   (02) 9264 3299
Fax   (02) 9264 1085

E-mail   virginia@afta.net.au
Internet   www.afta.com.au

President   Byron Roberts
Chief Executive Officer
            Susan Lenehan

AFTA STATE CHAPTERS IN:
New South Wales, Queensland, South
Australia, Victoria, Western Australia

AFTA Education and Training
Level 5, 120 Currie Street, Adelaide
SA 5000
Phone: (08) 8207 8643 Fax: (08) 8207 8457

The Australian Federation of Travel Agents (AFTA) represents the majority of travel agents in Australia. Members range from small independent agencies in regional and metropolitan areas to large retail groups, tour wholesalers, hotels, tour operators and various allied industry organisations.

AFTA provides pro-active representation of our members in industry and government affairs and acts as an information resource. Members are widely consulted on issues affecting them.

AFTA offers education and training to enhance the professionalism of our members and also offers courses to people interested in pursuing a career in travel.

AFTA encourages industry best practice amongst our members and promotes AFTA travel agents as providing the highest quality service to the travelling public. AFTA also plays a role in promoting travel and tourism generally.

Member Services
AFTA Travel Colleges
Insurances
Annual Convention
Awards for Excellence
Terms of Trade Guidelines
Industrial relations and legal advice, dispute resolution
Telstra flexiplan rebate scheme
Special merchant fees

AUSTRALIAN PETROLEUM PTY LTD
(TRADING AS AMPOL)

ACN 000 032 128

MLC Centre, 19–29 Martin Place
Sydney NSW 2000
GPO Box 3916
Sydney NSW 2001

Phone   (02) 9250 5000
Fax   (02) 9250 5297

E-mail   rtarnaws@ampol.com.au
Internet   www.ampol.com.au

Managing Director
            Dr I D Blackburne
Finance Director
            D J Mansour

Level 2, 39 Oxford Street, Epping NSW 2121
Phone: (02) 9855 2362 Fax: (02) 9868 4160

Level 7, 220 St Georges Terrace, Perth WA 6000
Phone: (08) 9261 2922 Fax: (08) 9322 2287

Level 17, 499 St Kilda Road, Melbourne VIC 3000
Phone: (03) 9279 9555 Fax: (03) 9279 9572

Level 13, 9 Sherwood Road, Toowong QLD 4066
Phone: (07) 3877 7442 Fax: (07) 3877 7514

With 62.5 per cent Australian ownership, Australian Petroleum Pty Ltd, trading as Ampol, was formed by the merger of Ampol and Caltex in 1995.

Ampol is the largest refiner/marketer of petroleum products in Australia, with operations in all States and territories.

Ampol is the largest fuel supplier for Qantas, supplying jet fuel for its aircraft, and diesel and lubricants for its 'on tarmac' fleet. Ampol also keeps the 'on road' fleet moving for Qantas with the Ampol Starcard.

AVIATION DISTRIBUTORS INC.

One Capital Drive
Lakeforest
CA United States 92630

Phone   (1) 714 586 7558
Fax   (1) 714 586 6246

Chief Executive Officer
          Osaman Bakhit
Executive Vice President
          Jeff Ward

Aviation Distributors (ADI) is one of the world's 10 largest aircraft parts redistributors and inventory management service providers to major commercial airlines worldwide.

ADI locates, acquires and supplies most parts and components found on commercial aircraft today including engines, cowlings, avionics, landing gear, wheels, brakes, hydraulics, interiors and galleys. Additionally, ADI engages in marketing agreements and consignment sales for commercial airlines, distributors and original equipment manufacturers.

ADI locates, acquires and markets parts from all major aviation manufacturers including Boeing, Airbus, Lockheed, McDonnell Douglas, General Electric, Pratt & Whitney and Rolls Royce. The company specialises in parts for the Boeing 737, 747 and 767 series, the Airbus 300 series and the McDonnell Douglas 80, DC and MD series aircraft.

ADI has a multilingual sales force of 27 representative in southern California and London. The sales force is organised by region with 10 representatives covering North America, five covering Europe, four covering Pacific Rim countries, three covering China, two covering the Middle East and three covering South and Latin America.

The company's sales representatives focus on developing and maintaining strong relationships with the airlines.

BAR CODE DATA SYSTEMS PTY LIMITED

ACN 002 370 452

Head Office
41–45 Lorraine Street
Peakhurst NSW 2210

Phone   (02) 9534 5888
Fax   (02) 9533 4605

E-mail   barcode@barcodedata.com.au
Internet   www.barcodedata.com.au

Managing Director
          Trevor W Dean
Director and Company Secretary
          Lesley M Dean
General Manager
          Michael Bayliss
National Sales Manager
          Ronald Abdy

Bar Code Data Systems Pty Limited (BCDS) was founded in 1982 and is a fully Australian-owned company. From day one the principal aim of the company was to act as a total data capture bureau, dedicated to every aspect of bar code systems and electronic automatic data capture technologies for government and industry. BCDS offer the widest selection of automatic identification systems in Australia, representing manufacturers from the United States, Europe, Japan and Taiwan. Products include bar code readers (including 2D), portable image scanners, bar code label and ID card printers, bar code printing consumables (ribbons and labels), magnetic stripe and smart card reader/encoders and SmartPoint miniature RFID tag readers. Clients are offered the very best equipment available for their specific applications. Services include EAN film masters, bar code label, tag and form printing, security ID plastic card printing (full colour) and swing tickets. Technologies available include radio frequency data capture, radio frequency identification tags, infra red data transfer, biometric (fingerprint scanning) and touch button security systems, and voice data entry.

Bar Code Data Systems are proud to be a supplier of automatic technology to Qantas.

ACN 004 085 616

360 Elizabeth Street
Melbourne VIC 3000
GPO Box 5222BB
Melbourne VIC 3001

Phone   (03) 9268 4111
Fax   (03) 9268 4478

Internet   www.bp.com

Chief Executive Officer Air BP International
          Ralph Alexander
Regional Asset Manager Australasia
          Tim Ind

BP AUSTRALIA LIMITED

Air BP, BP House, Breakspear Way, Hemel Hempstead, Herts HP2 4UL, United Kingdom
Phone: (44) 1442 22 5711 Fax: (44) 1442 22 4861

Air BP, 200 Westlake Park Boulevard, Houston, Texas 77079-2682 United States
Phone: (1) 281 560 3830 Fax: (1) 281 597 2186

Air BP is the international business unit within BP responsible for marketing aviation fuels, lubricants and specialist products and is the third largest aviation fuel supplier in the world.

Air BP is the oldest supplier of aviation fuels in Australasia (Australia, New Zealand and the South-West Pacific), where it now supplies aviation fuel at more than 150 locations through direct-into-plane operations at capital cities and a wide agency network.

Air BP sells fuel to international and domestic commercial passenger and cargo airlines. In addition, Air BP services the specialised needs of general aviation customers, ranging from heavy corporate jet operators to weekend pilots of small, single-engine piston aircraft. Its aviation activities range from state-of-the-art hydrant systems, to the provision of aviation fuels in drums to outback areas for bush pilot operators.

ACN 060 581 526

16–18 Waltham Street
Artarmon NSW 2064
PO Box 848
Artarmon NSW 2064

Phone   (02) 9437 4000
Fax   (02) 9906 5500

Director   George Tsivis
Director   Angela Sakellis

BROADLEX CLEANING AUSTRALIA PTY LIMITED

Unit 4, 14–18 Kembla Street, Fyshwick ACT 2609
Phone: (02) 6239 1635 Fax: (02) 6239 1194

91–97 Islington Street, Collingwood VIC 3066
Phone: (03) 9419 1803 Fax: (03) 9415 1569

Broadlex was established in 1969 to provide a high-quality cleaning service utilising the most cost-effective and advanced methods in cleaning. Broadlex is committed to expanding their business partnership with Qantas, to the benefit of both Qantas and Broadlex.

ACN 003 607 332

Unit 7, 2–4 Dunlop Street
South Strathfield NSW 2136
PO Box 190
Enfield NSW 2136

Phone   (02) 9742 5555
Fax   (02) 9742 5174

E-mail   broflo@broflo.com.au
Internet   www.broflo.com.au/

Chief Executive Officer
           Audrey M Murton
Director Operations
           John H Phillips

BROCHURE FLOW INTERNATIONAL LIMITED

Brochure Flow is proud to be associated with one of the world's best airlines, the internationally acclaimed Qantas!

Brochure Flow is a service provider to Qantas Airways and Qantas Holidays, and this partnership dates back 19 years.

Our services to Qantas Airways have passed through several of their notable milestones:

- Opening of the Big Apple Route;
- The non-stop flight from London to Sydney via the Kangaroo Route;
- Changeover from Trans Australia Airlines (TAA) to Australian Airlines and now Qantas—The Australian Airline;
- The 75th birthday celebrations of Qantas.

Brochure Flow pioneered professional distribution services to the travel and tourism industry Australia-wide. Today, Brochure Flow is synonymous with consistent high quality and competitiveness. Our services include collating, packaging and distribution, warehousing and inventory management, database management, Internet content provision, direct mailing, direct marketing consultancy and customer market support.

We enjoy a distinguished level of credibility and an enviable reputation not only in the travel and tourism industry but also in the corporate business world.

In this our 20th year of operations, we rededicate ourselves and our services to all our customers, large and small, in the travel and tourism industry, and the corporate business world.

ACN 004 213 692

Shirley Street
Granville NSW 2142

Phone   (02) 9682 0711
Fax   (02) 9682 0777

Internet   www.capral-aluminium.com.au

Chairman
           Jeremy Davis
Managing Director
           Ian Edwards

CAPRAL ALUMINIUM LIMITED

Capral Aluminium Limited is a substantial manufacturer of aluminium products, with assets of $800 million.

Capral's primary business consists of its aluminium smelter and trading operations. The company owns and operates a major smelter at Kurri Kurri in New South Wales.

The Extrusion Division produces a comprehensive range of extruded and drawn products for the building, transport and automotive industries.

The Sheet Division rolls ingot into a diverse range of plate, coil and sheet products for the building, transport and packaging industries.

The Foil Division processes coiled stock into plain and coated/laminated foil products for the pharmaceutical, confectionery, diary, food service and catering industries, and is the proud supplier of foil catering products to Qantas.

CARIBINER WAVELENGTH

CARIBINERWAVELENGTH PTY LIMITED

ACN 077 757 307

Level 2, 384 Eastern Valley Way
East Roseville NSW 2069

Phone   (02) 9417 1677
Fax   (02) 9417 1330

E-mail   info@wavelength.com.au
Internet   www.wavelength.com.au

Chief Executive Officer
               Paul Kenny
General Manager
               Karen Fawcett

CARIBINERWAVELENGTH PTY LIMITED

'The George', 129 Fitzroy Street, St Kilda VIC 3182
Phone: (03) 9593 8955 Fax: (03) 9593 8966

Suite 701, Kelvin House, 16 The Terrace, Wellington, New Zealand
Phone: (64) 4 473 8296 Fax: (64) 4 473 8298

7th Floor, 46 Lyndhurst Terrace, Central, Hong Kong
Phone: (852) 2805 1767 Fax: (852) 2805 1768

As a full service global business communications company, our mission is to help our clients achieve their business objectives by communicating more effectively with key external and internal audiences.

In addition to our communications strategy, creative and project management expertise, our in-house resources include a computer-based design, art and print team, multi-image and slide production, a video production department, a project management team and a fully equipped technical staging department. There are 68 full-time staff at CaribinerWavelength, operating out of Sydney, Melbourne and Wellington, New Zealand.

. . . We call it face-to-face communication.

CATHAY PACIFIC CATERING SERVICES

CATHAY PACIFIC CATERING SERVICES

Head Office
4/F, Block E, CPA Building
Hong Kong International Airport
Hong Kong

Phone   (852) 2747 3003
Fax   (852) 2325 5448

E-mail   cpcshq@cxair.com

Chairman   Patrick Tsai
Director and General Manager
               Andrew Herdman

CATHAY PACIFIC CATERING SERVICES

9th Floor, Block D, CPA Building, Hong Kong International Airport, Hong Kong
Phone: (852) 2747 3188 Fax: (852) 2765 7355

263–274 King Street, Mascot NSW 2020
Phone: (02) 9669 6800 Fax: (02) 9669 5372

444 Stuart Highway, Winnellie NT 0821
Phone: (08) 8947 0853 Fax: (08) 8947 0865

Cathay Pacific Catering Services specialises in providing high-quality inflight catering from our nine associated flight kitchens in Hong Kong, Taipei, Ho Chi Minh City, Osaka, Cebu, Sydney, Darwin, Toronto and Vancouver. We prepare over 80,000 meals per day for over 60 international airlines.

Cathay Pacific Catering Services is committed to providing consistent products and excellent services to Qantas and all our customers. We have greatly enjoyed working with Qantas, delivering quality meals to enhance its position as one of the world's leading airlines.

Congratulations to Qantas on its 50th anniversary of the Kangaroo Route, and wishing the airline every future success.

ACN 003 067 221

Unit 1, 1 Short Street
Chatswood NSW 2067

Phone   (02) 9417 5555
Fax   (02) 9417 2131

E-mail   bjburgess@ccs.net.au
Internet   www.ccs.net.au

Managing Director
           Brendan Burgess
Director   Brenda Burgess

CORPORATE COMPUTER SALES
(AUSTRALIA) PTY LTD

Corporate Computer Sales (CCS) is a privately owned Australian company specialising in the supply of computer and communications products and services to government and corporate organisations throughout Australia.

Founded in 1986, CCS has provided national coverage on products and services for its customers. It represents some of the world's largest information technology organisations, including Compaq, IBM, Microsoft and Novell. These established relationships enable CCS to deliver tangible value-added benefits to our customers.

A dedicated service team of systems engineers, plus an experienced account management team, provides our clients with a broad range of services in the networking, communications (Internet) and support environment, including the supply of hardware and software, business systems design and planning, project management, implementation, post-sales support and outsourcing of technical resources.

The benefits of CCS' 'total support' philosophy have resulted in an ability to build strong, long-term relationships with our clients. Such partnerships provide the foundation for CCS' continual growth into the next millennium.

300 West Service Road
Washington Dulles International Airport
Washington, DC 20041
United States

Phone   (1) 703 742 4300
Fax   (1) 703 742 4321

President   Patrick G Deasy
Executive Vice President
             Milagros Dedekind

DYNAIR GROUND SERVICES GROUP

- Largest independent ground handling company in America.
- Totally owned subsidiary of ALPHA Airports Group Plc.
- Established in 1949, McGuire Air Force Base, New Jersey.

DynAir Services provides airport handling services which include passenger, ramp, cleaning, reservations, ground equipment, aircraft line and onboard telecommunications maintenance, operations dispatch and load control, cargo warehousing and customer service, interline baggage, deicing, total quality management training, passenger screening and security, skycap, crew bus and limousine transportation.

DynAir handles more than 250,000 schedule and chartered flights per annum.

DynAir Fuelling provides into-plane fuelling, tank farm management, tank operation and maintenance, fixed base operations facilities and consulting services. DynAir Fuelling processes more than two billion gallons of fuel annually and into-planes 1,200 flights per day or 430,000 per year.

DynAir CFE handles over two billion pounds of cargo annually at more than 28 airports with extensive experience providing support services for the overnight cargo industry. DynAir CFE services more than 28,000 flights per annum.

GLIDEPATH LIMITED

ACN 065 210 540

30 Cartwright Road
Glen Eden Auckland
New Zealand 1007

Phone   (64) 9 818 3354
Fax   (64) 9 818 9994

E-mail   sales@glidepath.co.nz
Internet   www.glidepath.co.nz

Chairman   Ken Stevens
Chief Executive Officer
                  Neil Sayer

Glidepath Limited
Unit 3, 1 Coggins Place, Mascot NSW 2020
Phone: (02) 9669 1917 Fax: (02) 9669 1979

Glidepath Asia Pte Limited
Jalan Kayu Post Office, PO Box 53 Singapore 918002
Phone: (65) 266 1088 Fax: (65) 261 1828

Glidepath Limited is a world-class manufacturer of custom engineered conveyor systems, high-speed sorting and handling systems, and airport baggage handling systems. Glidepath manufactures baggage handling products ranging from small carousel and check-in conveyor installations in minor ports to large automated sortation baggage handling systems utilising IATA 10 digit licence plate technology in the major airports of the world. Glidepath's skilled engineers and designers, utilising the most modern computer aided and manufacturing systems, can undertake full turnkey systems including: research and development; design and drawing preparation; concept consulting and design; both mechanical and electrical manufacturing; site engineering and supervision; commissioning; and operation and maintenance programs. These products and services have been successfully used for 25 years, most recently on the Qantas Sydney Domestic Terminal and Qantas Melbourne Domestic Terminal.

Robertson

HH ROBERTSON (AUSTRALIA) PTY LIMITED

ACN 000 195 086

110 Pacific Highway
St Leonards NSW 2065
PO Box 454
St Leonards NSW 2065

Phone   (02) 9439 3777
Fax   (02) 9906 7961

E-mail   sales@robertson.com.au
Internet   www.robertson.com.au

Chief Executive Officer
                  Russell E Hill
General Manager, Pacific
                  Lester R Rundle

HH Robertson Singapore Pte Limited
51 Goldhill Plaza, #11–08/12 Newton Road, Singapore 308900
Phone: (65) 255 1622 Fax: (65) 254 1128

HH Robertson Hong Kong Limited
Suite 710, Ocean Centre, Harbour City
Tsim Sha Tsui, Kowloon, Hong Kong
Phone: (852) 2736 2070 Fax: (852) 2736 2150

At HH Robertson we develop building systems to the highest technical standards. We also design, engineer, manufacture, fix and warrant the systems we develop for our clients.

Through 90 years, our objective has been constant: to produce results on which our clients can depend—without fear of compromise.

From the beginning the Robertson name has been synonymous with innovation, professional service and quality throughout the Asia–Pacific region.

HH Robertson Asia–Pacific Group provides a complete range of design and engineering detailing, fabrication, supply and installation services supporting the construction of integrated architectural wall and glazing systems; single skin, built-up or panellised industrial roof and wall systems; and gravity ventilation systems and louvres.

These products and services are successfully brought together on such projects as the Qantas Sydney Domestic Terminal redevelopment.

HOLIDAY TOURS & TRAVEL PTE LTD

300 Orchard Road
The Promenade #07–01 to 10
Singapore 238861

Phone   (65) 734 7091
Fax   (65) 732 3497

E-mail   httsin@singnet.com.sg

Managing Director
           Choo Teck Wong, Dennis

Holiday Tours & Travel is a leading destination management company in the Asia–Pacific. We offer the benefits of a one-stop travel agency through our offices in Singapore, Thailand, Malaysia and Hong Kong.

We offer our customers the convenience of services such as ground transportation, meet and assist services, professional guides, daily sightseeing tours, hotel accommodation, tour desks, tour planning and car rentals.

Holiday Tours & Travel also have a department dedicated to managing conventions, conferences and exhibitions. Our commitment to high-quality customer service ensures that we go that extra mile to surpass the high expectations of our customers.

KPMG

45 Clarence Street
Sydney NSW 2000
PO Box H67, Australia Square
Sydney NSW 2000

Phone   (02) 9335 7000
Fax   (02) 9299 7077

Internet   www.kpmg.com.au

Chairman   John Harkness
Managing Partner, NSW
            Anthony J Clark, AM

KPMG has major accounting, tax, corporate finance and consulting practices in Australia and around the world. Partners and staff service clients across all industries and a wide range of services are available. KPMG acts as auditors, taxation, corporate and accountancy advisors to Qantas.

ACN 000 835 487

3 Thomas Holt Drive
North Ryde NSW 2113
PO Box 198
North Ryde NSW 2113

Phone   (02) 9805 5805
Fax   (02) 9805 0420

E-mail   marketing@mtxaspac.com.au
Internet   www.mtxaspac.com.au

Managing Director
             Chris Cheadle
Finance Director
             Paul O'Neill

MEMOREX TELEX PTY LIMITED
(A KANEMATSU COMPANY)

Memorex Telex Asia–Pacific have been business partners with Qantas for over 20 years and have provided value-added support services and products in that time. Memorex Telex Asia–Pacific is responsible for the integrity of business-critical equipment ensuring computer uptime is maximised and flight delays minimised.

Memorex Telex Asia–Pacific services are provided to Qantas internationally by teams of highly skilled computer industry professionals who are consistently achieving maintenance service levels in excess of 95 per cent for the maintenance of the Qantas computer network.

Memorex Telex Asia–Pacific is a progressive company with a well-defined business strategy that aligns them with business-critical organisations such as Qantas. The company's ambition is to ensure that Memorex Telex Asia–Pacific is the customer's *first choice* for business-critical information networks through the delivery of superior services, unsurpassed support and market-leading technologies.

ACN 003 433 234

Suite 2, 9–11 Montford Crescent
North Lyneham ACT 2602

Phone   (02) 6257 6873
Fax   (02) 6257 6976

E-mail   info@mercadier.com.au
Internet   www.mercadier.com.au

Managing Director
             John O'Neill
Director   Beverley Fenby

MERCADIER PTY LTD

Mercadier is a strong and well-balanced company offering support in the areas of management consulting, project management and software engineering. Our common theme is contributing to the strategic development of our clients.

Management Consulting services include performance management, survey/questionnaire development and analysis, program evaluation and review, change management, training and management development programs, and the preparation of high-level documentation and reports.

Project Management services include the determination of project organisational structures, the preparation and evaluation of proposals and tenders, conducting project performance audits and risk analysis.

Software Engineering services include the development of information systems or application software to support business processes, modelling human resource capabilities, remote vehicle tracking, the development and installation of Geographic Information Systems, the production of customised maps, and sales and support of specialised software for these areas.

Phoenix

your partner in computer personnel

ACN 003 921 355

80 Arthur Street
North Sydney NSW 2060

Phone   (02) 9957 4897
Fax   (02) 9922 1929

E-mail   reception@phoenix.com.au
Internet   www.phoenix.com.au

Managing Director
            Arthur E Cooley
Executive Director
            Barbara A Haig

PHOENIX CONTRACTING PTY LTD

332 St Kilda Road, Melbourne VIC 3000
Phone: (03) 9693 7530 Fax: (03) 9693 7590

Level 5, 33 Salamanca Place, Hobart TAS 7000
Phone: (03) 6224 3466 Fax: (03) 6224 2547

113 Wickham Terrace, Brisbane QLD 4000
Phone: (07) 3845 7500 Fax: (07) 3845 7555

Phoenix Contracting is a dynamic recruitment organisation, specialising in providing comprehensive Information Technology resources in the Asia–Pacific region.

We are part of the Global Diversified Services Group of the Fluor Corporation, through our parent TRS Staffing Solutions.

Our mission statement is to:
* provide our contractors and candidates with opportunities that best suit their skills, talents and goals;
* facilitate the take-up of these opportunities;
* offer the best contractors and candidates to our clients;
* outsource the non-core activities of our clients with our core skills and processes.

Phoenix is a preferred supplier to the New South Wales Government and a host of major companies and agencies.

Our total quality management system is certified to International Standard ISO9002.

ACN 006 810 368

387 Flemington Road
North Melbourne VIC 3051
PO Box 499
North Melbourne VIC 3051

Phone   (03) 9326 9544
Fax   (03) 9320 1244

E-mail   Polaris@Polaris.com.au
Internet   www.Polaris@Polaris.com.au

Managing Director
            Trevor Guest
General Manager
            Wayne Guest

POLARIS COMMUNICATIONS

Polaris Communications understands integration technology and the importance of customer service, and recognises the competencies required to make an organisation successful. As a supplier to Qantas, government agencies such as the Department of Social Security, and telecommunications giants like Telstra, Ericsson and Fujitsu, Polaris is renowned for its ability to exceed user expectations and provide the highest levels of service at all times. We are proud to be the endorsed supplier of Plantronics telephone headset products and other telecommunications services to such an array of leading Australian organisations and the Federal Government.

Since 1980 we have built our service from the ground up, based on our values of loyalty and integrity. Polaris now leads the way in the field of telephone headsets and, having been part of the distinguished Qantas supplier team for the past decade, our mission is to grow and prosper with our client partners as we meet the forthcoming technology challenges.

RATIONAL SOFTWARE CORPORATION PTY LTD

ACN 069 307 286

Level 13, Zenith Centre
821 Pacific Highway
Chatswood NSW 2067

Phone   (02) 9419 8455
Fax   (02) 9419 8466

E-mail   australia@rational.com
Internet   www.rational.com

Managing Director
                Jeff Pope
Financial Controller
                W Chow

Rational Software—Leaders in Component-based Software Development

Rational provides software to automate the development of component-based applications by integrating best-of-breed products in five areas of the software development life cycle: requirements management for capturing and managing the business objectives of a software system; visual modelling for creating a graphical blueprint of a software application and its components and interfaces, making it easier to understand and manipulate; automated software quality for automating time-consuming and error-prone manual testing procedures, resulting in faster delivery of high-quality software applications; process automation for providing guidance to software managers and developers about how to create software as a competitive business asset; and software configuration management for helping project teams manage software changes.

**Information Delivery
Software**

SAS INSTITUTE AUSTRALIA PTY LTD

ACN 002 287 247

300 Burns Bay Road
(Private Bag 52)
Lane Cove NSW 2066

Phone   (02) 9428 0428
Fax   (02) 9418 7211

E-mail   info@oz.sas.com
Internet   www.sas.com

Managing Director
                Brian Wood
Deputy Managing Director
                Bill Gibson

Other offices located in Melbourne,
Brisbane, Canberra and Perth.

Now in its 21st year, SAS Institute is the largest privately owned software company in the world. Recent research has shown that 97 of the top 100 US Fortune 500 companies are SAS Institute customers. Confirming SAS Institute's preferred software supplier status, Qantas won the 1997 Enterprise Computing Award for the strategic use of the SAS System at SUGA '97 (SAS Users' Group Australia).

   SAS Institute is the leading global software developer of enterprise-wide information delivery systems and has established itself as a leader in the data warehouse and data mining markets. It is a wholly owned subsidiary with over 800 licensed sites nationally within several key markets, including banking and finance, insurance, utilities, manufacturing, government and health.

   1996 revenues were over US$600 million and represent the Institute's 20th consecutive year of double digit growth. SAS Institute continued its strong annual growth in Australia with new business surging up to 54 per cent and revenues totalling $21 million.

THE SHELL COMPANY OF AUSTRALIA LIMITED

ACN 004 610 459

1 Spring Street
Melbourne VIC 3000
GPO Box 872K
Melbourne VIC 3001

Phone   (03) 9666 5261
Fax   (03) 9666 5917

Chairman and Chief Executive Officer
      Roland Williams
Executive Director Oil Products
      Peter Duncan

Shell, like Qantas, has a history in Australia which goes back to the early days of aviation. Shell spirit was used in many early pioneering flights, like the Smith Brother's flight in 1919, Amy Johnson's historic first solo flight by a woman pilot, and the first mail flight by Charles Kingsford Smith—all flights made from England to Australia.

Shell has grown through the years to become the world's leading supplier of aviation fuels—Shell Aviation offers refuelling services at over 800 airports in 80 countries around the globe.

Shell is proud to have been there in the beginning when Qantas started operations in Longreach, Queensland, and we are proud to have remained a major supplier of the 'flying kangaroo' in the 1990s, both in Australia and overseas.

SIAM INTER•CONTINENTAL BANGKOK
'The Business Resort in the Heart of Bangkok'

967 Rama I Road
Pathumwan
Bangkok 10330
Thailand

Phone   (66) 2 253 0355–7
Fax   (66) 2 253 2275

E-mail   bangkok@interconti.com
Internet   www.interconti.com

Regional Vice President Operations and
      General Manager
            Eduardo Fahrenkrug
Resident Manager
            Juan Carlos Diago

Providing for the wellbeing of the frequent traveller requires insight, dedication and, above all, leadership.

For the past 50 years, Inter•Continental Hotels and Resorts has built a reputation for innovation in the hospitality industry. By carefully combining our international experience with the local cultures of our host cities, we have earned a worldwide reputation for providing exceptional accommodation in more than 70 countries.

In Thailand we are especially proud to have the Siam Inter•Continental. Set in the midst of a 26-acre botanical garden, the hotel simply offers the best of both worlds.

With a reputation for the best service in the city, where better to choose when travelling to the 'Land of Smiles'.

TELSTRA CORPORATION LIMITED

ACN 051 775 556

Head Office
242 Exhibition Street
Melbourne VIC 3000
Locked Bag 6531
Sydney NSW 1100

Phone	(03) 9634 1111
Fax	(03) 9364 6778

E-mail	sgosling@ncagccsu.telstra.com.au
Internet	www.telstra.com.au

Chairman
          David M Hoare
Chief Executive Officer
          W Frank Blount

Sydney Office
320 Pitt Street, Sydney NSW 2000
Phone: (02) 9298 9015 Fax: (02) 9298 9020

United Kingdom Office
1st Floor
14 Buckingham Gate, London SW1E 6LB United Kingdom
Phone: (44) 171 828 2328 Fax: (44) 171 828 7938

Telstra is a leading provider of electronic communications and information services in Australia and the Asia–Pacific region, and is a significant global supplier.

TFK CORPORATION

New Tokyo International Airport
Narita City
Chiba Pref
Japan 282
PO Box 126
Narita City
Chiba Pref
Japan 282

Phone	(81) 476 32 5558
Fax	(81) 476 32 5586

Chairman	Susumu Ashino
President	Tsutomu Nomaguchi

Dedicated to serving the airlines of the world, the name of TFK has been linked with Qantas for the past 35 years.

Building on in-flight catering experience, TFK also operates two hotels and three restaurants in the Narita Airport vicinity.

THAI AIRPORTS GROUND SERVICES CO., LTD.

171 Cargo Terminal 4
Bangkok International Airport
Vibhavadi Rangsit Road
Donmuang
Bangkok 10210 Thailand

Phone   (66) 2 535 1986, 535 5600,
             996 8064
Fax   (66) 2 535 1987

President and Chief Executive Officer
        Anuphong Rojnuckarin

Thai Airports Ground Services Co., Ltd. (TAGS) is proud to have been associated with Qantas since our inception on 1 July 1990. From humble beginnings in an airfreight facility of 8,000 square metres, handling 10 airlines, we have now grown to serving 22 airlines from a premises with a total area in excess of 40,000 square metres and investments in freight handling systems alone exceeding US$20 million. Qantas continues to be ranked within the top five clients in terms of freight tonnage and flights handled. Total tonnage handled through our facilities is approximately 170,000 tons per annum, growing at a rate of 17 per cent per year.

As the first ground handling agent in the world to have received ISO9002 certification in all operations divisions, we continue to meet and exceed all our clients' quality expectations, all made possible by the faith and support Qantas has shown and given us all these years.

Our best wishes to everyone at Qantas on this auspicious occasion!

THE MILLENNIUM GLOUCESTER LONDON

Harrington Gardens
London SW7 4LH United Kingdom
Phone   (44) 171 373 6030
Fax   (44) 171 373 0409

HEAD OFFICE
Millennium & Copthorne Hotels Plc
Victoria House
Victoria Road
Horley Surrey RH6 7AF United Kingdom
Phone   (44) 1293 77 2288
Fax   (44) 1293 77 2345

E-mail   marketing@mill-cop.com
Internet   www.mill-cop.com

Chairman   Kwek Leng Beng
Managing Director
        John O'Shea

The Millennium Gloucester London is the only European hotel to support *The Longest Hop— Celebrating 50 Years of the Qantas Kangaroo Route 1947–1997*.

In presenting our congratulations to Qantas on its 50th anniversary of the Kangaroo Route, we look forward to a further 50 years of a rewarding relationship with all our guests who are Qantas passengers.

We have invested some £20 million in making your stay in London an experience worth travelling halfway around the world for.

TRAFALGAR TOURS

ACN 000 717 715

'Tracon House'
27 Belgrave Street
Manly NSW 2095

Phone   (02) 9977 9202
Fax   (02) 9977 9295

Managing Director, Australia and
    New Zealand
             Peter J Elkins
Director   Anthony J Carolan

This year Trafalgar Tours celebrates its golden anniversary, having grown from a small tour operator to one of the world's largest and most successful tour companies.

Motorcoach touring has changed dramatically over the past five decades. With Trafalgar's established quality, reliability and value, and international infrastructure, clients are assured of memorable holidays that far exceed their expectations. As many of our existing passengers know, touring Britain and Europe by motorcoach, accompanied by an experienced tour director, enables them to meet new people from around the world. It removes the worry and stress, offers the added advantage of specially reserved hotel accommodation each touring night, in addition to included sightseeing and shopping, as well as free time. Last but not least, it provides total security and peace of mind while travelling from one destination to another in our care.

Trafalgar Tours . . .
First choice for the quality you want, at an affordable price.

TURBINE OVERHAUL SERVICES PTE LTD

No 5 Tuas Drive 2
Singapore 638639

Phone   (65) 862 1001
Fax   (65) 862 1068

E-mail   kyap@pweh.com

Managing Director
             Jeremy Chan

Singapore-based Turbine Overhaul Services (TOS) is a joint venture between Pratt & Whitney (P&W), a division of United Technologies, and Singapore Technologies Aerospace (STAe). The company specialises in the repair and overhaul of gas turbine blades and vanes, with current repair capability well extended to the following turbine blades and vanes:

- Pratt & Whitney PW4000 series;
- Pratt & Whitney PW2000 series;
- Pratt & Whitney JT9D series;
- Pratt & Whitney JT8D series;
- CFM International CFM56 series Low Pressure.

TOS is fully equipped with the latest and most sophisticated equipment and technology. The company has been operating for 15 years and is the market leader in its own right. As a result of TOS's continuous efforts to improve its quality and performance, and upgrade its technical capabilities, its clientele list has increased to over 100 worldwide, including 36 of the world's leading airlines.

THE WESTIN STAMFORD
& WESTIN PLAZA
Singapore

2 Stamford Road
Singapore 178882

Phone   (65) 338 8585 main
           (65) 339 6633 reservations
Fax   (65) 338 2862 main
           (65) 336 5117 reservations

E-mail   westinl@singnet.com.sg
Internet   www.westinsingapore.com

Managing Director
           Bernard Agache
Director of Marketing
           Christine Hodder

THE WESTIN STAMFORD & WESTIN PLAZA

The Westin Hotels are designed as part of the Raffles City Complex which comprises The Westin Stamford, The Westin Plaza, Raffles City Convention Centre and the Raffles City Shopping Centre.

Standing at 226.13 metres (735 feet), The Westin Stamford is listed in the *Guinness Book of World Records* as the tallest hotel in the world.

The Westin Hotels are located in the heartland of Singapore. Just 20 minutes from Changi Airport, the hotels are set in one of the oldest historical districts of Singapore. The Mass Rapid Transit (MRT) station, City Hall, which is one of the two major interchanges between the north–south and east–west lines, is at the doorstep of the hotel complex.

The Westin Hotels offer guests the choice of 11 restaurants and lounges; a fitness centre which includes two free-form swimming pools, a jacuzzi, two indoor squash courts, six tennis courts, a gymnasium, sauna, steam room, whirlpool and massage rooms; a business centre; and the Raffles City Convention Centre—one of the largest convention centres in Singapore.

Perched at the top of the world's tallest hotel, The Westin Stamford, are 29 palatial and luxurious penthouse suites—The Stamford Crest. These deluxe suites offer the best in elegance, luxury and comfort as well as a spectacular vista of the island.

ACN 051 992 226
19 Buffalo Road
Gladesville NSW 2111
PO Box M53
Monash Park NSW 2111
Phone   (02) 9844 6111
Fax   (02) 9844 6161
E-mail   phones@abtc.com.au
Internet   www.abtc.com.au
Director   Peter George
Managing Director
             Michael Teear

ACN 008 682 957
9 Subway Road
Rockdale NSW 2216
PO Box 105
Rockdale NSW 2216
Phone   (02) 9556 1666
Fax   (02) 9556 1566

Chairman   John Cambridge
Director   Robert Barnwell

ACN 000 013 098
4–6 Elva Street
Strathfield NSW 2135
PO Box 118
Strathfield NSW 2135
Phone   (02) 9746 0444
Fax   (02) 9746 1479
E-mail   mailbox@snpsecurity.com.au
Internet   www.snpsecurity.com.au
Managing Director
             Kevin Roche, OAM
Directors   Peter Roche, Tom Roche

AUSTRALIAN BUSINESS TELEPHONE COMPANY PTY LTD

52 Pelham Street, Carlton VIC 3053
Phone: (03) 9663 6868 Fax: (03) 9663 1013
Unit 6/121 Newmarket Road, Windsor QLD 4030
Phone: (07) 3861 0099 Fax: (07) 3861 0188

ABTC specialises in the marketing, distribution, sales and service of peripheral telephone products. ABTC's Leader Product Portfolio is quite extensive, with a range of telephones and headsets tailored to meet most applications in the business, travel and hospitality marketplaces.

The range includes basic wall phones, standard and on-hook telephones, conference telephones, telephones specifically designed for headset operation and, most importantly, telephones that cater almost exclusively for the travel and hospitality industry—the Teledex range of telephones—phones that have been adopted as the de facto standard by many global hotel chains.

BARNWELL CAMBRIDGE PTY LTD

Barnwell Cambridge Pty Ltd is an electrical contracting and engineering company engaged in all facets of maintenance, commercial, industrial and refurbishment installation work. The company has earned a reputation for quality workmanship having successfully undertaken numerous complex installations requiring expertise in co-ordination and programming of services. Directors maintain a hands-on approach to the day-to-day operations.

Our company has maintained a continuous presence on the Sydney Jet Base and peripheral centres, assisting Qantas maintenance staff in the installation and servicing of electrical services to the administration, aircraft maintenance and flight services facilities to meet the stringent procedures required by Qantas, and to ensure, in part, the maintenance of their enviable safety record.

Congratulations Qantas.

SNP SECURITY

SNP Security is the largest privately owned and operated Australian security company in the commercial security service industry.

Established in 1923, SNP Security (formerly Sydney Night Patrol) provides professional security services to the commercial, private, government and manufacturing sectors.

Our services include: aviation security; alarm installation and monitoring; on-site guards; undercover investigations; access control; and building management systems. SNP is the exclusive Australian business partner for Casi-Rusco, the world's largest access control supplier.

SNP is a quality endorsed company to ISO9002, Licence No 10113.

SNP is in business to create and keep clients and this is achieved by being proactive to our clients needs and building on the relationships we have created.

SNP is proud to have been a service provider to Qantas since the commencement of passenger screening at Sydney International Airport in the early 1970s.

BIBLIOGRAPHY/ACKNOWLEDGEMENTS

Affleck, Arthur H, *The Wandering Years*, Longmans, 1964.

Allan, G U, with Shearman Elizabeth, *Scotty Allan*, Clarion, 1993.

Bennett-Bremner, E, *Front-Line Airline*, Angus & Robertson, 1944 (Qantas Founders Outback Museum edition, 1996).

Betts, Ed, 'The Original Connies' (three parts), *AAAHS Journal*, American Aviation Historical Society, 1991.

Burgess, Colin, *50 Years of Service, the Story of Qantas Cabin Crew*, published in *Transit* and other forms by Qantas Cabin Services, 1988–90.

Clune, Frank, *High-Ho to London*, Angus & Robertson, 1948.

Fysh, Sir Hudson, *Qantas Rising*, Angus and Robertson, 1965.

Fysh, Sir Hudson, *Qantas at War*, Angus and Robertson, 1968.

Fysh, Sir Hudson, *Wings to the World*, Angus and Robertson, 1970 (Qantas Founders Outback Museum edition).

Gunn, John, *The Defeat of Distance (Qantas 1919–1939)*, University of Queensland Press, 1985.

Gunn, John, *Challenging Horizons (Qantas 1939–1954)*, University of Queensland Press, 1987 (paperback edition 1990).

Gunn, John, *High Corridors (Qantas 1954–1970)*, University of Queensland Press, 1987.

Gunn, John, unpublished mss (Qantas 1971–1988), retained by Qantas, completed c. 1990.

Harris, Max, and Burgess, Colin, *Laughter in the Air*, Hutchinson, 1988.

Millers Guide 1995, Miller Form, Moonee Ponds, Victoria, 1995.

Qantas News, numerous issues c. 1940–c. 1996, Qantas Public Affairs.

Qantas news releases, Qantas Public Affairs, c. 1970–1995.

Sims, Charles, 'London–Sydney Return', The *Aeroplane*, London, (two articles during 1948).

The *Sydney Morning Herald*, microfilm editions August 1945–August 1948 (courtesy State Library of NSW).

Thomas, Greg, and Whelan, Col, *Schweppes Rugby '97*, Mandarin (Reed Books Australia), 1997.

Wyndham, Captain Ian, 'The Constellation Era: Circling the Globe', article prepared for *Qantas News*.

Thanks to Barry Masters of Tennis New South Wales.

Extensive use was made of press clippings and other information maintained by Qantas, Mascot, including files of timetables and aircraft and radio technical manuals, which are too numerous to detail. The assistance of Captain Ian Wyndham, retired engineer George Roberts, Ted Malmgren and the late Ern Aldis, OBE, together with other retired Qantas crew and ground staff, is gratefully acknowledged.

PHOTOGRAPHIC CREDITS

Photographs supplied by Qantas Airways Limited.

SUPPORTING PHOTOGRAPHY

Australian Picture Library/Corbis Bettmann, pp. 18, 35, 39, 62, 63.

Halmarick/The Fairfax Photo Library, pp. 24–25.

The Photo Library—Sydney/Hulton-Getty, pp. 36, 65.

The Photo Library—Sydney/Doug Armand, p. 61.

The Photo Library—Sydney/Steven Rothfeld, p. 64.

The Photo Library—Sydney/Joel Simon, p. 65.

The Photo Library—Sydney/Steve Lissau, p. 66.

The Photo Library—Sydney/Pete Seaward, p. 123.

© Julian Green, pp. 133, 137, 143.

Portraits by James Manning, pp. 38, 48, 60, 70, 94, 114, 128, 134.